OLD
TESTAMENT
WORDS

Also from Chalice Press by Mary Donovan Turner

Saved from Silence: Finding Women's Voice in Preaching
(with Mary Lin Hudson)

OLD TESTAMENT WORDS

REFLECTIONS FOR PREACHING

MARY DONOVAN TURNER

CHALICE
PRESS

ST. LOUIS, MISSOURI

Biblical quotations, unless otherwise noted, are from the *New Revised Standard Version Bible*, copyright 1989, Division of Christian Education of the National Council of the Churches of Christ in the United States of America. Used by permission. All rights reserved.

Cover art: © PhotoDisc, Inc.
Cover design: John Grizzell
Interior design: Elizabeth Wright
Art direction: Michael Domínguez

This book is printed on acid-free, recycled paper.

Visit Chalice Press on the World Wide Web at
www.chalicepress.com

10 9 8 7 6 5 4 3 2 1   03 04 05 06 07 08

Library of Congress Cataloging–in–Publication Data

Turner, Mary Donovan.
  Old Testament words : reflections for preaching / Mary Donovan Turner.
    p. cm.
Includes bibliographical references and index.
    ISBN 0-8272-2714-0 (alk. paper)
1. Bible. O.T.—Homiletical use. 2. Preaching. I. Title.
    BS1191.5.T87 2003
230'.0411—dc21   2003007880

Printed in the United States of America

To Pat, Bob, Jim, and Jerry
and their families…
You know how much you mean to me

To Lamar, Chris, and Erin
For forever supporting all that I do

Contents

Acknowledgments

We can never know who has helped us become who we are, who has influenced the words we try so desperately to put on the page. Friends, colleagues, teachers, ministers, parishioners, parents, siblings, aunts and uncles, nieces and nephews, spouse and children—you are all here... somewhere.

Writing does not come easily to me, and so I am grateful beyond words for the support many have so generously given so that this volume could come into being. Dr. Jon L. Berquist, at Chalice Press, encourages, listens, and challenges. I am glad that he is not only my editor but also my friend. Dr. Archie Smith, Jr., read early drafts of the volume and lent a helpful perspective for each word, a perspective born out of his own context and background, a perspective that both reinforced and challenged my own. Thanks to Audrey Englert for her editorial and secretarial help and to the many work-study students who have assisted her throughout the last semesters. Karen R. reminded me in early conversations that there was another way to view the world, and Elisabeth Middelberg faithfully served as my research assistant, trying mightily to organize my work.

I remain grateful to the students, staff, board members, and faculty of Pacific School of Religion, who support my teaching and scholarship. They have been a part of my life for over a decade; they have taught me and enabled me to grow.

Introduction

I have long been intrigued with the Old Testament. In my early childhood I, along with many other children, relished the sights and sounds of its stories that stimulated our imaginations and entertained us. Who would not find interesting the idea of a small, helpless child cradled in a basket riding the waves and ripples of a large African river? Or a very large boat protecting all God's creatures from a relentless storm—long-necked giraffes and laughing monkeys alike? I was not immune to the Israelite storytellers' genius.

As time went by, however, I gradually became aware of the complexity of this collection of narratives and laws and poems and proverbs and oracles we call the Old Testament, or perhaps the First Testament, or the Hebrew Bible. It was evident not by the conversations about it, but by the way many churches avoided it, that these words were too serious or frightening or perhaps even offensive for the likes of a church member like me. Being naturally curious, however, I wanted to make decisions about this testament's value or lack of it for myself. Spurred on by excellent Old Testament professors in undergraduate and graduate studies, the adventure of exploring and trying to come to understand the history and literature and faith journey of a people spanning nearly a millennium has not been lost on me. I have been captured by the Old Testament—sometimes positively engaged by it, sometimes offended. I have often had to wrestle certain texts to the ground. At times the sheer beauty of the words has thrilled me or comforted me. I have often been, perhaps like you, puzzled or perplexed. And yet I am convinced that this collection of books from Genesis to Malachi is worthy of more than a glimpse or moment of our time. Locked away in the world of Hebrew thought and language we will find the God we worship come to life in some surprising and challenging ways. We will find this God's nostrils flaring with anger at the injustice done to small, vulnerable children. And we will find this same God bending down and, with love like the most nurturing and caring parent among us, refusing to let us go. There is no discerning with certainty or total clarity who this God is. Even the names of this God are "slippery" and ambiguous. (Sometimes the divine name in the Old Testament is Yahweh; this is translated Lord in the NRSV. Sometimes the name is El or Elohim; this is translated God.) What we thought we knew perhaps will be challenged. What we did not know will, I hope, be brought forth in a way that will educate and also inspire.

Perhaps what we will find on our adventure will be consistent with your own ways of understanding and interpreting God's presence in our lives and in the world. But perhaps it will not. The Old Testament was written by scores of men, and perhaps women, whose life contexts were radically different from our own. Still, we can learn an enormous amount from their own struggles to find the words that could, even in small ways, begin to describe the God with whom they were in relationship and whom they could not fully understand. Their stories are troubling and challenging, but sometimes in their earthiness and struggle they mirror our own. It is fascinating to realize that might be so.

This adventure could take many forms. We could begin to explore the Old Testament's varied cast of characters, or we could analyze the plots of the narratives as they begin to unfold before us—family narratives and narratives of the nation. But instead, I have chosen to talk with you about words. Just words. Single, solitary words that in large or small measure are the "building blocks" of the many theologies the Old Testament holds. I have chosen, with a great deal of difficulty, thirty-eight words. There are many more possibilities—scores of them. Some might wonder about the choices I have made. I am aware that these choices are not the ones a Jewish rabbi or someone steeped in the Jewish faith would make. Neither are these necessarily the Hebrew words found most frequently in our Old Testament text. Only a very few of them will be familiar, most likely, in their Hebrew form. *Shalom* is an obvious exception! But coming to understand these thirty-eight words, I believe, will open new horizons for us, will offer up to us important questions and issues related to faith. We will begin to wonder how these Hebrew words and ideas helped form and fashion the thoughts of New Testament communities and writers. And we will begin to see how variegated and strange and wondrous the world of the Old Testament can be.

Every chapter of the thirty-eight in this volume will be headed by the Hebrew word under discussion and a phonetic guide so that you can begin to learn, pronounce, and speak it. For those who have had some training in Hebrew, this might serve as a handy reminder if linguistic skills have tarnished or rusted with age. Whether you are an accomplished Hebrew scholar past or present, or whether this world of Hebrew—where words are read "backwards"—is completely new and foreign to you, linger with each entry for a while. See it and hear it and read about it. Be open to the challenges you'll find. And if you are an avid student of the biblical text or a preacher, the index at the conclusion of the book will lead you to sources that will help you find the chapters and verses in the Old Testament where each word is found. The study questions will help you explore the meanings of these words with those in your own local context. Perhaps new theological understandings will open to you. That is my hope.

In this volume, we will consider some of the ways in which these words were used by the early Christians who wrote the books we now call the New Testament, and we will also investigate another interpretive tradition that held the Hebrew Bible/Old Testament writings as sacred—the rabbinical traditions of the early centuries C.E.[1] The rabbis' probing questions, keen insights, and delightful imaginations have the power to challenge and instruct and entertain us. We will learn from them. I myself am an ordained minister in the Christian Church. That perspective forms and fashions in conscious and unconscious ways the words I have chosen and the information I have decided to share about them. I have seen this volume as one way to expand the conversation in the Christian community about the Old Testament and preaching. It is one of my favorite conversations, and I would like for it to be one of yours. I would like for this to be a grand invitation to reconsider the richness of Old Testament narrative. Just like the God it describes, perhaps you will find that this testament's thirty-nine books will just refuse to "let you go." May it be so.

(Pronounce "or")

Light

Let there be light! Perhaps you can remember your first serious encounters with this phrase and the creation stories of the first three chapters of Genesis. Even a casual read of the rhythmic depiction of the beginning of the universe in chapter 1 and the story of the creation of the earth and Adam and Eve in chapters 2—3 elicit an intriguing set of questions and inconsistencies. Why does the creation story in chapter 1 use one name for God *(Elohim)* while the creation story in chapters 2—3 use another *(Yahweh)*? Why does the order of creation differ between the two? Why does God refer to God's self as "we"? What does it mean in the story that as both male and female we are created in God's image? What does the second creation story really say about women and their roles in life, work, and the world? And how, we wonder, could God have created light on day 1, yet the sun and moon and stars find themselves much further down the creation chain?

While each of these questions and the multitude of others that arise from the reading of the seventy-nine verses of Genesis 1—3 are important, it is the last one that commands our attention here. In answering the question of how light and the sun could be created on different days, we come to understand more fully the use of the metaphor of light in the Old Testament.

Consider these points: (1) Long before the sun can be seen making its way over the eastern horizon in Palestine, light shines, and dawn has broken. (2) While the light shines during the day, the moon and stars shine in the night, and the night is still filled with darkness. (3) On cloudy days when the sun is not visible, the world is still filled with light![1] It makes sense, then, that the connection in the ancient world between light and sun would not be automatic or taken for granted. It was the coming light, not the sun, that meant that the mysterious but consistent cycle of evening and day, evening and day was again fulfilled. It was this daily cycle on which the Hebrews depended, and while we are not so fully conscious of it, we too completely trust this cycle of day and night. It orders our existence. Thus, light in the Old Testament is not the sun. The sun brings warmth perhaps, but it is the morning that brings the first rays of light. In the Old Testament, to experience the light means that one is alive. To be born is to have the opportunity to see the light. An increase in the "light of the eyes" means an increase in vitality and joy. When the "light of the eyes" fails, a person approaches death. Those who have lived and then died see the light no more.[2]

To understand *light*, it is helpful for us first to understand our thoughts and feelings about the darkness of night. Perhaps nighttime brings to mind the pleasantness of rest, or perhaps moments of anxiety and fear. Perhaps in the night the way is not so clearly set forth before you, and you imagine yourself stumbling clumsily as you try to reach your destination. Your steps are hesitant and very cautious; your arms are held out in front of you lest you unknowingly run into an unseen obstacle. Your thoughts about night are, perhaps, ambiguous, and if they are, they are consistent with the varied thoughts and feelings about night in the Old Testament. One thing is clear. It is *not* in the night that salvation visits us. It is symbolically at dawn that salvation comes. This understanding that God's mercies are "new every morning" (Lam. 3:23) inspires our zealous singing of these words from the refrain of "Great Is Thy Faithfulness":

"Morning by morning new mercies I see. All I have needed thy hand hath provided."[3] In the morning, when life is re-created, the powers of chaos are averted yet one more time, as they were on that first day of creation, and we are renewed. "[God's] appearing is as sure as the dawn" (Hos. 6:3). That's Hosea's way of speaking to this same reality.

"We are walking in the light of God, we are walking in the light of God."[4] We often sing these words in the Pacific School of Religion chapel, always with a great and mighty enthusiasm. I think we are not fully aware of what we are potentially claiming as we sing. To walk in the light of God according to Hebrew thought means to walk in God's paths through the shadows cast by our living. It means to keep walking even if the night seems too long. It means claiming by faith that even the night can be "luminous." It means we are walking the path that brings us all to well-being and salvation. In this way, walking in the light can be seen as the goal for our human existence. It is not simply a gift we receive, this light in which we have the privilege to walk. Often in the Old Testament, the law or wisdom sheds this light on our way. It is instruction, and it is our search for under-standing that sheds light. It is through study that God reveals the "deep and mysterious" things about existence, and we learn to live life in relation to God and one another.

In the Old Testament those who choose to walk in this light live in contrast to the sinners or those who do not know light, who rebel against it. At night they devise evil plans; they carry them out in secret. No one can see them, not even God. They are "friends with the terrors of deep darkness" (Job 24:17), and it is out of the night darkness that they make their attacks against the righteous. Knowing this, we can understand the exuberance of the prophetic word found in Isaiah that describes the future hopes and possibilities for a nation that now lives in distress and anguish.

> The people who walked in darkness have seen
>   a great light;
> those who lived in a land of deep darkness—on
>   them light has shined. (9:2)

The new day dawns.
I will lead the blind by a road they do not know,
by paths they have not known I will guide
    them.
I will turn the darkness before them into light.
    (42:16)
The new day dawns.
Arise, shine; for your light has come, and the
    glory of the LORD has risen upon you.
For darkness shall cover the earth, and thick
    darkness the peoples;
but the LORD will arise upon you, and [the
    Lord's] glory will appear over you. (60:1–2)

The new day dawns, and all the terrors and fears that seem to loom larger than life in the night hours diminish as the faint rays of light begin to beam their pinkish threads across the sky. First, Second, and Third Isaiah (chapters 1—39, 40—55, and 56—66, respectively) all use this magnificent image of the breaking of day to bring a word of hope and salvation. This is, no doubt, the image in the mind of the psalmist when he sang, "Yahweh is my light and my salvation." (Ps. 27:1). Salvation is symbolically related here to God's very first good act of creation.

The Jewish rabbis speak poignantly about the light; it is a powerful metaphor for God and for the Torah, the first five books of the Old Testament. There is a tale about a man who is walking through the dark woods one night, alone and afraid. He is walking slowly and carefully. As he is walking, another man joins him, and this man leads the way with the aid of the lantern that he carries. They come to a crossroads and part company. The second continues on, moving forward easily. The other must slow down and once again grope his way through the darkness. The story teaches about the importance of carrying one's own light, but not an external light. It speaks about the importance of carrying an internal light, the light of God and Torah. When one is aware of the light and open to the assistance of this illumination, one never has to be afraid of walking in the darkness.[5]

One strand of Judaism (the Hasidic)[6] teaches that each of us has an internal light, a Holy Spark of the Divine, but that we don't always see it or allow it to be seen. Our inner lights, our sparks, are like diamonds. If the diamond is buried in the ground, it cannot show its luster. No matter how deeply it is buried, the Holy Spark still resides within. This tradition speaks about a healing of the world when the sparks that are scattered and dispersed because of our own sin are collected and vessels are put back together again. Good replaces evil, and the complete Light of God will be revealed.[7]

As a constant and recurring reminder of the light of the world, the Friday night Sabbath candles in a Jewish home bring peace, connection to the past, and potent reminders of the importance of God to life.

(Pronounce "oh-yev")

Enemy

There are no nations without enemies, and enemies are created in a multitude of ways and for a variety of reasons. A nation can be a perceived enemy because it is powerful and poses a constant threat to another's good health and well-being. It has the potential to oppress. Or a nation can be an enemy because it has control over a resource that is desired or needed by others. Or a nation can be an enemy simply because the language spoken is "different" or because its people have a different color of skin stretched over their bones. Or perhaps over the centuries stories have accrued about times and people and places when one nation was at "odds" with the other, and the memories cannot be forgotten. Animosity grows; hatred builds. And enemies continue being enemies.

It is not surprising that the small nation of Israel, nestled at the edge of the Mediterranean Sea, had its enemies. Not because it had a great power to oppress, of course, but because it lay there at the crossroads of mighty empires who needed clearance through its borders and thus its allegiance. Dwarfed by the empires around it, Israel and its leaders turned to their God to help them survive.

Often when the Old Testament authors speak of enemies, it is this kind of enemy that commands their attention—the nations all about, those filled with people who worshiped the wrong god, those who were not obedient to nor awed by Yahweh. Egypt was the enemy because Egypt had oppressed the Israelites and made them their slaves. The warring tribes that they encountered on their forty-year adventure in the wilderness were their enemies. Those who inhabited the country of Palestine when the Israelites made their entrance there were enemies. They already inhabited the land of "milk and honey," the land the storytellers suggest the Israelites had been seeking to claim as their own. And as the kingdoms of Israel and Judah went through a series of rulers on their thrones, they were pushed and pulled about by the nations who wanted something from them; those nations were the enemies.

And so it is not surprising that in the Old Testament narratives and songs the community tells stories and sings about the enemies (there are nearly seventy-five references to enemies in the psalms alone!). The psalms that sing about the trials and exploits of Israel's kings often speak of enemies. "Your arrows are sharp in the heart of the king's enemies; the peoples fall under you" (Ps. 45:5). The superscription of Psalm 18 indicates that this is a song David sang when he was delivered from the hand of his enemies and from Saul. The psalm expresses love for Yahweh, who is strength, rock, fortress, deliverer, shield, horn of salvation, and stronghold. The psalmist had called upon Yahweh so that he could be saved from the enemy (18:3). Yahweh reached down, drew him out of the mighty waters, and delivered him from the strong enemy who hated him (v. 17). Yahweh made the enemies turn back (v. 40). And as the psalm comes to closure, the affirmation is once again reinforced: Yahweh lives…the one who delivers the psalmist from his enemies (vv. 46–48).

The psalms are filled with references not only to national enemies but also to personal ones. Scholars have frequently asked, "Who are these enemies?" But no single theory seems to account for the complexity of the individual laments or the descriptions of each one's despair. In some, the enemy seems to be some kind of disease. In others, the enemy seems to be someone who attacks the credibility of or ridicules the lamenter. Probably many enemies plague those who sing, and the ambiguity allows us the opportunity to identify the enemies in our own lives. Perhaps a memory. A regret. A fear. A secret. A habit…

We can tell something about the work of "enemies" in the psalms by identifying the verbs that describe their work. Enemies oppress, are hostile to, smite or strike, pursue or persecute, deal treacherously, deceive, exalt themselves, make themselves great, scoff and revile, rejoice, open wide their mouths, or ridicule. They gnash with their teeth. We understand the people and things that do these to us. In the psalms the enemy is the one who lives beyond the border, the aggressor, the one who desecrates the holy places of Yahweh (the most holy of places), or the devious one who feigns friendship or loyalty or honor. The enemy is often described as animal—as less than human; enemies are like the lurking lion or the dog that devours its prey.[1]

We understand the words of the "enemy psalms"; we ourselves have been the targets of aggression. We have been abandoned and betrayed. We have been humiliated. It takes little to remind us of the powerful emotions that these engender inside us. These psalms can be a source of embarrassment when they are prescribed for our liturgies, or if not embarrassment, concern. The stringent calls for Yahweh to help destroy the enemy or the radical cries for vengeance on the enemy leave us in an important theological quandary about prayer, about God's love for all creation, even about violence.

All my enemies shall be ashamed and struck with terror.(Ps. 6:10)

When my enemies turned back, they stumbled and perished before you. For you have maintained my just cause.(9:3–4)

How long, O LORD? Will you forget me forever? How long will you hide your face from me? How long must I bear pain in my soul, and have sorrow in my heart all day long? How long shall my enemy be exalted over me? (13:1–2)

What are the ways that we as a community of faith can deal thoughtfully and responsibly with these calls for the enemy's demise? It is probably wise for us to acknowledge first the strong emotions witnessed in these psalms and ask ourselves where in our own worship lives we allow the expression of such strong, intense emotion and lament. When do we name the things that oppress and ridicule and revile us? Reading the psalms presents a good opportunity to ask ourselves where in our lives we feel such hatred and anger. Where does it reside within us? We must not allow ourselves to be untouched by the psalms' passion. If we see the psalms as not prescriptive of life (things that prescribe the way life should be) but descriptive (things that describe the way the life is and the ways we are), we can use their readings confessionally and ask ourselves when it is that we make such distinctions between ourselves and the "other." When do we see good as "us" and evil as "them," sacred as "us" and profane as "them," innocent as "us" and guilty as "them"? Do we see ourselves as the pure, the righteous, the honest, the ones with integrity?[2] These psalms can call us again to recognize the dignity of every person created in the image of God. And above all, it can be helpful to remember that the expression of this kind of emotion is healthy for us.

To express anger and even rage against those who persecute us does not mean that violence will be carried out toward them. Perhaps, even, the expression of that anger could prohibit the expression of violence and counterviolence in our world.

In Psalm 18, Yahweh has delivered David from the enemy because Yahweh is the deliverer and the source of strength. But the picture, of course, is much more complicated. The attacks of the enemies on Israel can be seen as manifestations of divine punishment brought about by Yahweh. God gives the Israelites into the hands of the enemies and sometimes even into the "lands" of the enemies. Later, it is God's gracious hand that gathers them back. Yahweh has promised to protect them when they are faithful. And when they are not, Yahweh calls another nation or allows another nation to have control over and destroy the Israelite people.

At a time when the well-being and prosperity of a people were dependent on their relationships with the nations around them, it would not be surprising that their understanding of the world and of God would be seen through the lens of these relationships. When they are free and prosperous, God is with them. When they are persecuted or ripped from their homeland and taken into exile, God is not. When they are obedient, God is with them. When they are not obedient, God is not. And perhaps it is not only that God is not with them; perhaps God is against them. God becomes the enemy (see, for instance, Lamentations 2). God has that much power.

There is no doubt, however, that as the story of the conquest is told, as the Israelites move from the wilderness into the land of Canaan, and as the monarchy is established, the hope for them is that they will have rest from the enemies around them.[3]

> When you cross over the Jordan and live in the land that the LORD your God is allotting to you, and when he gives you rest from your enemies all around you so that you live in safety… (Deut. 12:10)

> And now the LORD your God has given rest to your kindred, as he promised them. (Josh. 22:4)

> A long time afterward, when the LORD had given rest to Israel from all their enemies all around... (Josh. 23:1)

> Now when the king was settled in his house, and the LORD had given him rest from all his enemies around him... (2 Samuel 7:1)

It is in dealing with the enemy that the Israelites feel a great weariness, and it is Yahweh whose power can provide rest for them. Second Isaiah so eloquently brings that assurance to his audience:

> The LORD is the everlasting God, the Creator of
> the ends of the earth.
> He does not grow weary;
> his understanding is unsearchable.
> He gives power to the faint, and strengthens the
> powerless.
> Even youths will faint and be weary,
> and the young will fall exhausted;
> but those who wait for the LORD shall renew
> their strength,
> they shall mount up with wings like eagles,
> they shall run and not be weary,
> they shall walk and not faint.
> (Isa. 40:28b-31)

Perhaps it is to this understanding of the God who longs for us to be free from weariness that the writer of Proverbs relates: "When the ways of the people please the LORD, he causes even their enemies to be at peace with them" (Prov. 16:7).

Exodus 23:4–5 reads, "When you come upon your enemy's ox or donkey going astray, you shall bring it back. When you see the donkey of one who hates you lying under its burden and you would hold back from setting it free, you must help set it free." The rabbis tell a story to illustrate this law. Two travelers who hated each other were going down the road. The beast of one was lying down under its great burden. The other traveler first passed him by, but went back and lent a hand. He helped his enemy in loading and unloading. He began talking to his enemy, "Release a bit here, pull up over there, unload over here." Then peace came between them so that the one with the overloaded beast said, "Did I not suppose that he hated me? But look how compassionate he was with me." Eventually the two entered the inn, and ate and drank together and became fast friends. What caused them to become friends? Because one of them kept what was written in the Torah.[4]

It is a difficult thing, showing compassion to an enemy. "Who is the mightiest of the mighty?" one rabbi asked. "The one who can turn an enemy into a friend."[5]

(Pronounce "aph")

Anger

"Anger is cruel." "He that is soon angry acts foolishly." "Whoever is slow to anger has great understanding." "Make no friendship with an angry man." "The wise turn away anger." These sayings are, no doubt, what many of us would expect the biblical text to say about anger. We would expect admonitions to keep our anger "in check" and not to let our passions rule. We would expect to be instructed that patience is virtuous and that, to live life fully or wisely, our anger should be discounted, repressed, or turned away. And in some sense, it is true. The wisdom literature of the Old Testament, through pithy proverbs, says these things about anger. The partial quotations from Proverbs above illustrate this quite clearly. The later rabbis studying these proverbs also thought a great deal about human anger. "He who succumbs to anger succumbs to bad judgment."[1] "Do not seethe with anger and you will not sin."[2] "A man with a bad temper achieves nothing but his bad temper."[3] "There are three kinds of men whose life is not life: those who are too compassionate, those who are too prone to anger, and those who are too fastidious"[4] And when the disciples of a rabbi asked him, "To what do you attribute your long life?" He answered, "I never lost my temper in the midst of my family."[5]

We ourselves know, however, that anger is not as simple as that. It is strong, and as a strong emotion it is neither good nor bad in itself. There can be healthy and unhealthy expressions of it. It can be used to warn others about danger. It can be used as a pretext to attack or can harm another. Or, conversely, it can serve as a stimulant to protest injustice. It can be an appropriate response to loss and grief; it may be an important part of the grieving process. It can be rational or irrational. The sources of anger can be in the past or in the present. To recognize our anger can be an important part of our development. The rabbis recognized this ambivalence about anger in their recognition that every trait of personality must be manifested at the right time and in appropriate measure *(midah)*. Even anger. "Long ago I conquered my anger and placed it in my pocket. When I have need of it, I take it out," a rabbi said.[6] The rabbi perhaps was speaking something about *midah*—moderation. Positive and negative emotions may serve a very good purpose—in moderation.[7]

The attitudes about *'aph* in the Old Testament are more complicated than this. First, it is helpful to realize that many Hebrew words are translated "anger." One means something akin to curse, one to be excited, one to be hot, to glow or burn or tremble. But the word under consideration here, *'aph*, is interesting because it can be translated either "nostril" (nose) or "anger." Why this is so is not entirely clear. Perhaps it is because when one is angry there can be evidence of heavy breathing. Or perhaps when a person is angry her nostrils flare. Whatever the reason, the nose plays a peculiar role in the Old Testament's description of anger. For example, see Psalm 18:7–8: "for he was angry. Smoke rose up in his nose" (author's translation). This quotation describes Yahweh's overwhelming anger at the plight of the worshiper in the "snares of death," overwhelmed by the enemy.

This description of Yahweh is far from unusual. This particular word for anger (and the related *'appayim*) describes human anger 40 times in the Old Testament, but 170 times it describes divine anger. More than four times as often! This is a burning, smoking kind of anger. Of course, all sorts of things make God angry. God gets angry at the people God has created. Sometimes they are worshiping other gods, sometimes treating one another unjustly. Sometimes with a sense of pride and independence they delude themselves into thinking that they need to be in relation with God no longer. God gets angry at those who have forgotten that they are in a covenant relationship with the God who created them. God is angry when Moses is hesitant to take on the role as leader of the people, when the most vulnerable are exploited, when the Israelites whine and complain in the wilderness.

Yes, God is depicted as an angry God. But another strong thread runs through the text. This God is one who tries to control and suppress anger. God's anger is a last resort. This reality is given expression in a statement found with slight variations in several places in the Old Testament canon.

> The LORD is merciful and gracious, slow to anger and abounding in steadfast love. (Ps. 103:8)

> For I knew that you are a gracious God and merciful, slow to anger, and abounding in steadfast love, and ready to relent from punishing. (Jon. 4:2)

In the latter story, because Jonah knew from the beginning that this is a slow to anger, gracious God, Jonah avoided the calling to deliver a word of destruction to the Ninevites. He knew that the steadfast love of God would prevail, that this angry God is also a *patient* God who will wait and hope that people will consider their sins and repent. The rabbis talked about this patience in this way: They said that before God destroyed the world through the flood, God gave the people a very, very long time to repent and improve their ways. That is why there were ten generations between Adam and Noah. God kept waiting for repentance. Things went from bad to worse, however. Still, God did not bring the flood until God had given them a further chance to heed Noah's warnings. For 120 years Noah continued to preach and to rebuke them. Then Noah took a very long time building the ark. He first planted the cedar trees. "Why are you planting those saplings?" people would ask him. "To build the ark," he would answer. The people would scoff as he watered the trees and as they grew. Finally they were big, and Noah cut them down and built the ark. When the people would not end their scoffing and repent of their wickedness, God commanded Noah to bring his family and the animals into the ark. The time for the flood had come.[8]

The rabbis knew what Jonah had known: This God was a patient God. And so Jonah was left to struggle with this complex God filled with both *'aph* and compassion. It is difficult to understand. But Judaism, as the later rabbis indicated, was a religion that could hold together this seeming contradiction. The rabbis wondered, To whom does God pray? And what does God pray? This is the prayer the rabbis believed God addressed to God's self: "May it be acceptable before me, may it be my will, that my compassion may overcome mine anger, and that it may prevail over my justice when my children appeal to me, that I may deal with them in mercy and in love."[9]

The breath that comes through the nostrils to bring life is also the breath that flares out into the world bringing death and destruction. A mature understanding of God deals with these complexities. God is all of this.

(Pronounce "ay-pher")

Ashes

In many Christian communities the Lenten season begins with the ritual celebration of Ash Wednesday. Indications are that as early as the eighth century, on this occasion the worshiping community would approach the altar, and there the priest, dipping his thumb into the blessed ashes, would mark their foreheads with the sign of the cross, saying the words: "Remember [man] that thou art dust and unto dust thou shall return." The ashes used in the ceremony were made by the burning of the remains of the palms used in the Palm Sunday celebration the year before.

The earliest origins of this custom cannot be definitely recovered, but the long history of associating the ashes with repentance is clearly attested. It can be a powerful and meaningful ritual, perhaps because of the association of ash with fire that no longer burns. Cold ash seems to carry within it no hope of renewed flame or passion, or the ash brings to mind the related system of images in the Old Testament that are associated with profound loss, grief, or tragedy. Those images are ashes, sackcloth (a coarsely woven fabric made from animal hides), and fasting.

When we look through the Hebrew concordance, we find this word used about twenty times (often paired with a word that sounds much like it, the word for "dust"). That is not many, but the ash and the profound hurt and grief that it symbolizes are related to stories of the most tragic nature:

In 2 Samuel 13 we find the story of Tamar, desired and seduced by Amnon, her brother. Through a premeditated act he has his sister called to his bedside, where he is feigning illness. He asks that she bring him food. Tamar takes dough, kneads it, makes cakes, and bakes them. Amnon asks her to "lie with him." She refuses because she would not know how "to carry the shame." But Amnon, being stronger, rapes her and sends her away. In her shame, Tamar puts ashes on her head and tears the long robe she is wearing. Putting her hand on her head, she cries and goes away (2 Sam. 13:19).

In another tragedy, Job is first afflicted by Satan with loathsome sores from the sole of his foot to the crown of his head. He tries to scrape them off with the jagged edge of broken pottery. In his despair, he sits among ashes. Later, he describes the internal turmoil of one who is ridiculed and mocked by those around him.

> "And now my soul is poured out within me;
>   days of affliction have taken hold of me.
> The night racks my bones, and the pain that
>   gnaws me takes no rest.
> With violence he seizes my garment; he grasps
>   me by the collar of my tunic
> He has cast me into the mire, and I have
>   become like dust and ashes." (Job 30:16–19)

Job's life itself is symbolized by dust and ashes and the profound despair they represent. In the end (42:6), dust and ashes become the symbols for Job's repentance.

In Jonah, the Ninevites hear the word of the prophet who has been called by God to proclaim to them a word of impending destruction. Forty days more, and Nineveh shall be overthrown! The people believe the word that Jonah has delivered to them. They call for a fast and for sackcloth. The king puts on sackcloth and sits in ashes as an outward manifestation of what he has come to know (Jon. 3:6). The people of Nineveh are an evil and violent people; Jonah's fear is that God will relent and not exercise his fierce anger.

In Genesis Abraham describes himself as one who is but dust and ashes (Gen. 18:27). This signifies his mortality and humility before God.

The one who has seen God's affliction describes his experience this way in Lamentations 3: "[God] has made my teeth grind on gravel, and made me cower in ashes; my soul is bereft of peace; I have forgotten what happiness is; so I say, 'Gone is my glory, and all that I had hoped for from the LORD'" (Lam. 3:16–18).

In the book of Esther, when Mordecai realizes that King Ahasuerus has signed an edict and ordered the destruction of the Jewish community, he tears his clothes and puts on sackcloth and ashes. He wails with a loud and bitter cry. And there was a great mourning among the people with fasting and weeping and lamenting; they lay in sackcloth and ashes (Esth. 4:1–3).

The psalmist knows of disease that wastes his body, that makes his bones burn like a furnace. His skin clings to his bones; he is alone and is derided by his enemies. He calls out and says: "For I eat ashes like bread, and mingle tears with my drink" (Ps. 102:9). Misery is all he knows.

Together these paint a compelling portrait of at least part of the human condition. We know shame. We know about unjust persecutions. We know about evil and violence and the need to repent from them. We know about misery and despair. Ashes symbolize human frailty. The Hasidic rabbis taught that we must remember this frailty. "Everyone must have two pockets, so that he can reach into the one or the other according to his need. In the right pocket are the words, 'For my sake the world was created.' In the other, 'I am earth and ashes.' Each of us is thus created in the image of God and endowed with divinity by virtue of his or her soul. Each of us is also limited by our mortality and must concede that we came from dust and will return there."[1]

The Old Testament does not leave us in this despair; despair does not have the final word. Interestingly, the two texts that are chosen as possible Old Testament readings for Ash Wednesday (Joel 2:1–2, 12–17 and Isa. 58:1–12) both call us out of our lament and sadness about the world's plight. Joel calls the community to return to Yahweh with fasting and weeping and mourning. But he tells them to "rend your hearts and not your clothing" (Joel 2:13). It is not enough to lament our condition; we must have a change of heart and thus a change in the way we live.

Likewise, in Third Isaiah the prophet calls out to those who participate in the rituals of fasting. It is not enough to fast if on that day you serve your own interests and oppress your workers. It is not enough to lie down in sackcloth and ashes. A true ritual of repentance is reaching out to loose the bonds of injustice, to undo the thongs of the yoke, and to let the oppressed go free (Isa. 58:3–6). It is not enough to lament the terror; we must work to eliminate it! Thus, the ashes indicate the desire not only to acknowledge guilt but also to effect a true atonement to God and God's ways in the world. As our society becomes more secular and champions the winner and the hero, the set of symbols around Ash Wednesday become ever more foreign. Yet the ritual may hold the key to our redemption (the reversal of the values that help to destroy life and oppress others). It is to this place of radical recommitment that the ashes are intended to take us.

(Pronounce "eh-retz")

Earth, Land

God called the dry land "earth." According to Genesis 1:9, on the third day of creation God gathered together the waters under the sky so that dry land could appear. From the earth, plants and trees began to sprout. It was all very good. This first use of the word *'eretz* brings to the fore one of the meanings of this very important word, which is used more than 2,400 times in the Old Testament.

First, the word means "earth" in the cosmic sense. It, along with the heavens, make up the whole world—thus the common phrase in the Old Testament "the heavens and the earth." That means everything! This word for earth can also mean simply the ground on which people and things stand; it is the place where the dust lies and where creeping things creep. On it fall the dew and the rain, captured birds. On it sits the mourner; one bows toward it or prostrates oneself on it. It can open and swallow people; it can shake.[1] The earth was created by God, and thus, it belongs to God. "The earth is the LORD's and all that is in it, the world, and those who live in it; for [God] has founded it on the seas, and established it on the rivers" (Ps. 24:1).

When the word *'eretz* is used to designate a certain region or "land," interesting theological implications come into play. In Deuteronomy 26 we read a short historical credo, a very brief recounting of the history of the Israelite community and a remembering of the ways that God has guided them and been with them on their journey. The credo begins in verse 5: "A wandering Aramean was my ancestor; he went down into Egypt and lived there as an alien, few in number, and there he became a great nation, mighty and populous." The credo goes on to relate a brief account of the exodus and the deliverance through the sea. Then it recounts that God "brought us into this place and gave us this land, a land flowing with milk and honey" (v. 9). In response to the goodness of God, the firstfruits of the harvest are set down before God.

It is this understanding of the land, the land that God has given, that dominates the telling of the story of the conquest. The boundaries of this land are first spelled out in Genesis 15 when the promise is made to Abraham—a promise of a land and descendants without number. It is a holy land because it is a land created by God and given by God to the people. The promise is then articulated again to the matriarchs and patriarchs of the faith. It is with mixed feelings that we read in Joshua that the Israelites move into this land already occupied by the Canaanites and Perizzites and others to claim it as their own. The ongoing political struggle over the land bears witness to the long-standing importance of coming to understand the promise of the "land" in the Old Testament.

The word "earth" is not used simply to talk about that which is beneath our feet. It is used by Third Isaiah to bring the word of hope and promise about the age that is to come: "For I am about to create new heavens and a new earth; the former things shall not be remembered or come to mind. But be glad and rejoice forever in what I am creating; for I am about to create Jerusalem as a joy, and its people as a delight." (Isa. 65:17–18). The Jerusalem that had been devastated will, in the future, be rebuilt. Its future is filled with promise. There will be no more tears there, no more distress. It is this kind of future hope that sustained the community during its time of exile and despair. And perhaps each of us now holds a vision of what a "new earth" could look like.

(Pronounce "aysh")

Fire

Judgment. Life. Protection. Fire is a complex symbol in the Old Testament. It appears in the Hebrew narrative more than 375 times and symbolizes the ongoing relationship and conversation between God and humanity in all its varied manifestations. Fire often symbolizes God's revelation to us;

through sacrifices of fire, it symbolizes the human's approach and response to God. The covenant that Abraham makes with God is sealed by a flaming fire that moved between the separated pieces of animal (Gen. 15:17). It is a pillar of fire that guides the Israelites by night as they make their way through the wilderness to the land of promise (Ex. 13:21, 22; 14:19–20). Fire is an important element in the vision Ezekiel has as he stands among the exiles by the river Chebar (1:4, 13, 27).

Yahweh appears to Moses in a flame of fire, a bush that is not consumed, and calls Moses to go to Egypt to deliver the Israelites from slavery (Ex. 3:1–10). This theophany, God's making God's self known, is an intriguing story that has captivated the imaginations of its readers since it was first told. There was a fire. There was a bush. But the fire did not consume it. Why was God made known this way? Why through a bush? Why this kind of bush? Why to Moses? What did God say? What did God mean? What did Moses say in return? The rabbis asked interesting questions and gave interesting answers. Why was Moses chosen? Because he demonstrated as a shepherd such compassion for his sheep that God knew that he would make a good shepherd for Israel.[1] Why did God choose a thorn bush for the sign? To teach us that no place on earth, not even a thorn bush, is devoid of the presence of God.[2] And why did God call out the name of Moses two times without stopping between the calling of the names? Because a person with a heavy burden cries out in one breath.[3]

Nowhere in the Old Testament are references to fire more concentrated than in the Mount Sinai stories found in Deuteronomy (twelve citations in chapters 4 and 5 alone). In chapter 4 Moses is calling the people to remember the moment that the covenant with God was made, a story he wants them to remember so that they can tell it to their children and to their children's children. Remember, he tells them, that the mountain was ablaze with fire (Deut. 4:11). Remember that Yahweh spoke out of the fire (v. 12). He tells them not to make any graven images, because Yahweh their God is a devouring fire, a jealous God (vv. 23–24). Has any person ever heard the voice of God out of a fire and lived? Then in chapter 5, when the story is retold yet again, Moses reminds the community that Yahweh has spoken to them face-to-face out of the fire (v. 4). And it is this thought, not of Yahweh speaking, but of Yahweh speaking out of the fire, that frightens them, that causes them to ask Moses to go up the mountain and receive the word for them. It is the flaming voice of God that unnerves them (vv. 25–27). The fire has the potential to consume and destroy.

It is an unsettling image after all. The voice is intimate, personal, recognizable. To be in relationship through "voice" implies the closeness that is demanded for hearing. Intertwined with this portrait of an intimate, speaking God is this image of fire so potentially threatening and destructive. The community is at the same time drawn forward to listen and repelled because of potential danger.

The psalmist understood the devastating potential of Yahweh's fire. Fire and water are both images used to depict the anger Yahweh experiences.

> Then the earth reeled and rocked;
> > the foundations also of the
> > > mountains trembled
> > and quaked, because he was angry.
> Smoke went up from his nostrils,
> > and devouring fire from his mouth;
> > glowing coals flamed forth from him.
> > > > > > (Ps. 18:7–8)

It is not surprising that this imagery that associates Yahweh's anger with fire is found scattered about in the oracles of judgment and doom delivered by the Old Testament prophets. Here, the anger often burns so hotly that the prophet wonders and the community wonders if the fire can ever be contained.

> By your own act you shall lose the heritage that I gave you, and I will make you serve your enemies in a land that you do not know, for in my anger a fire is kindled that shall burn forever. (Jer. 17:4)

It is not always the judgment of God that flame and fire symbolize. Sometimes it is simply the power, the greatness of God who has control of something that seems to be uncontrollable. The psalmist, in describing the greatness, honor, and majesty of God, says, "You make the winds your messengers, fire and flame your ministers" (Ps. 104:4). Even these are used by this God who is greater than anything.

The Old Testament prophets were persons called forth to speak against religious and political establishments. Their words are often introduced by a messenger formula, "Thus says the Lord," which both claims God's authority and explains their compulsion to speak. The covenantal relationship between God and people—I am your God, and you are my people—undergirds their words of judgment and redemption. They borrow oral and literary forms of expression and use metaphors that grow from their everyday experiences to stir the moral imagination and invite a lived response from their hearers.

Prophets were called forth in a particular context to name the realities of life and interpret them from a theological perspective; they were interpreters of the national story. Prophets were mediators between God and humanity, consultants to kings, and preachers to the religious and political establishments. Their words were sometimes heavy and ponderous, calling the community back to covenant and right relationship with a just and holy God. Sometimes they were called to speak a word of comfort to a wayward, persecuted, and forgetful people. The prophets spoke paradoxical and perplexing words, hard words, and often at their calling they were clearly reminded that the role of prophet is not an easy one and not to be taken lightly. Of the 378 times the word *fire* is found in the Old Testament, 47 of them are in Ezekiel, 39 in Jeremiah, and 33 in Isaiah. Fire symbolizes the anger of God against the community, but in Jeremiah it also symbolizes the demanding nature of this calling; the prophet is to become the fire of God.

Therefore thus says the LORD, the God of hosts:
Because they have spoken this word, I am now

making my words in your mouth a fire, and this people wood, and the fire shall devour them. I am going to bring upon you a nation from far away, O house of Israel, says the LORD. (Jer. 5:14–15)

Who, then, are the prophets among us today? Who are those that keep reminding us how our ways of living do not meet the just and righteous standards God has for us? Whose words "burn"? Whose words act as a "refining fire," trying to melt away what is not good and productive in our communities of faith and our world? The prophetic task is ofttimes a lonely and dangerous one. Who is taking the risk to lead us to healthy and more life-giving ways?

(Pronounce "bah-rah")

To Create

A story is told about a heathen who approached a rabbi and asked him, "Who created the world?" The rabbi answered that God had created the world. The man asked, "What proof do you have?" The rabbi told him to come back the next day for proof. When the man returned the next day, the rabbi said to him, "That's a nice coat you are wearing. I wonder who made it." The man replied that the tailor had made it. The rabbi asked, "What proof do you have that the tailor made it?" And the man answered, "What sort of question is that? Everyone knows that a tailor makes clothes!" "In the same way," said the rabbi, "you can now understand that God created the world." When the man left, the rabbi said to his disciples, "Just as the existence of a house points to the builder who built it, and the clothes point to a tailor who sewed them, and the furniture to a carpenter who made it, so the existence of the world is proof in itself of an Almighty God who created it." This story speaks clearly to the understanding that there is one God who created all there is.[1]

In the beginning God created...As readers of the Old Testament, we are very familiar with this first expression in the canon. But perhaps we have not known that it is only God who could have created! God is always the subject of this verb, and it is always Israel's God. No foreign deity ever creates. Thus, the word stands for the creative agency and energy of God. God creates the heaven and the earth, people, Israel, and wonders, and brings about something new that has never been before. The word refers to "God's extraordinary, sovereign, both effortless and full free, unhindered creation."[2] God creates newness in the community. God also creates newness in the individual. This is so beautifully illustrated in the longings of the singer in Psalm 51: "Create in me a clean heart, O God, and put a new and right spirit within me. Do not cast me away from your presence, and do not take your holy spirit from me. Restore to me the joy of your salvation, and sustain in me a willing spirit"(Ps. 51:10–12).

It is the prophet Isaiah who calls most frequently on creation language to describe what God is doing and will do in the world. Second Isaiah (Isaiah chapters 40–55) shows the readers the power of the God who holds the future of the community; God is able to deliver. "The LORD is the everlasting God, the Creator of the ends of the earth. He does not faint or grow weary; his understanding is unsearchable." (Isa. 40:28). The people will be able to draw on the power of the one who created them, who created everything. "He gives power to the faint, and strengthens the powerless. Even youths will faint and be weary, and the young will fall exhausted; but those who wait for the LORD shall renew their strength, they shall mount up with wings like eagles, they shall run and not be weary, they shall walk and not faint" (40:29–31). Endurance to withstand and the hope that redemption will come can be offered only by this one God.

Throughout the sixteen chapters of Second Isaiah are reminders that the one who speaks to them is the Creator of the world—the ends of the earth (Isa. 42:5), the community and nation (43:1, 15), the heavens (44:24; 45:12, 18), the water (45:8) even darkness and evil (45:7). Everything has been made by God.

Third Isaiah (Isaiah chapters 56–66) also uses the creation imagery to describe what will be. For Jerusalem and its people—who have experienced devastation, loss of land and religious symbol, exile, and despair—among them God will be creating a new thing. "For I am about to create new heavens and a new earth; the former things shall not be remembered or come to mind. But be glad and rejoice forever in what I am creating; for I am about to create Jerusalem as a joy, and its people as a delight" (Isa. 65:17–18). The exuberance comes from knowing that a better day is ahead when the One who longs to create new life lives among us.

(Pronounce "b'reeth")

Covenant

If we began reading the Old Testament in Genesis 1:1, we would first find the word *b'rith* when reading the stories about Noah and his family. God looks down on the earth and discovers that it is corrupt and filled with violence. God has determined to "make an end to all flesh," but directs Noah to build an ark to house his family and the earth's animals while a flood of waters comes to destroy everything else now living. And then God says to Noah, "But I will establish my covenant with you; and you shall come into the ark, you, your sons, your wife, and your sons' wives with you" (Gen. 6:18).

When the floodwaters subside and the family walks on the dry land, again the covenantal promise is made. "As for me, I am establishing my covenant with you and your descendants after you, and with every living creature that is with you...I establish my covenant with you, that never again shall all flesh be cut off by the waters of a flood, and never again shall there be a flood to destroy the earth" (Gen. 9:9–11). A bow is set in the clouds to be a reminder that the promise has been made. "Never again" is the promise. Never again.

God makes other covenants, of course. God makes a covenant with the patriarchs beginning with Abraham. The covenant includes the gift of the land (Gen. 15:18; Ex. 6:4), the promise of descendants (Gen. 17:2), and the promise to continue to be their God (Gen. 17:7). The covenant established with David includes the assurance that David's throne will always be occupied by someone in the Davidic line (2 Sam. 7:16).

The reader of Genesis encounters the first of the ancestors of faith in the story of the call of Abraham in chapter 12. The first eleven chapters of Genesis have to do with the world. They recount stories of creation and flood and tower, and they deal with the lives and fates of all peoples. Suddenly, then, as chapter 11 comes to an end, the focus narrows, and we "zoom" in on the face of a single person: "Now the LORD said to Abram..." The following verses go on to recount the call of Yahweh to this solitary individual to leave his country and his extended family to go to a new place. An unfamiliar place. An unknown place. We as readers are curious about this one named Abram, as we are about all the individuals with whom God "cut a covenant" (the expression often used to indicate that a covenant was being made). Why Abram? Out of all the people who live in the world that has been created, why this one?

There is only one tiny clue in the Old Testament. It comes in the book of Joshua. Joshua, recounting for the community the words of Yahweh, says "Your ancestors lived of old beyond the Euphrates—Terah, the father of Abraham and of Nahor; and they served other gods. Then I took your father Abraham from beyond the River and led him through all the land of Canaan" (Josh. 24:2–3, author's translation). There is the slightest indication here that the family of Abraham served many gods but that Abraham was somehow different. Somehow even then Abraham knew about the one God of what was to be Israel. Out of the interpretation of these few verses came a very large and tenacious interpretive tradition that honors Abraham as one who believed in the one true God.

There are many stories from the rabbis about the childhood of Abraham. We wonder about the great women and men of faith, those about whom we know nothing or little until as adults they enter the biblical narrative and play their parts. The rabbis tell a story of Abraham working as a youth in the market where his family sold the images they had made of other gods. A man came to Abraham in the marketplace and said, "Have you a god to sell?" "What kind?" Abraham asked. "I am a mighty man," he answered, "so give me a god as mighty as I." Abraham gives him the god sitting highest on the shelf. The man pays, and as he leaves, Abraham asks him, "How old are you?" The man says that he is seventy years old. Abraham responds, "Woe to a man who is seventy but worships a god who was made only today."[1]

Even as casual readers of these stories of our ancestors, we wonder about this word *covenant* and what kind of promise or agreement is being made here. What kind of relationship is being established? What kind of bond is being forged? Where did this word *covenant* come from? What does it mean? Some of these questions can be answered by looking at the many usages of the word in the Old Testament. But some of the answers to these questions are locked away and are not accessible to us.

There are many theories about the meaning of the word *covenant*; the word has commanded a great deal of attention from Jewish and Christian scholars alike. Some have thought that the word was originally related to the word for "eat" or "dine." If so, it would refer to the meal that accompanied a covenantal ceremony. Some have thought the word could be related to other ancient Near Eastern words meaning "between" or "among." Another plausible explanation is that it is associated with the words meaning "clasp" or "fetter." In this way, *covenant* would have something to do with a bond, like a treaty made between nations. It is this possibility that has commanded the greatest amount of attention.

Covenant in the Old Testament has to do with a formal agreement or treaty between two parties, with each party assuming some kind of commitment or obligation toward the other. This might be a commitment made between two individuals, such as David and Jonathan (See 1 Samuel 18:3; 20:16), or between different nations, such as between Abraham and Abimelech, king of Gerar (Gen. 21:31). A covenant could also be imposed by a greater power on a lesser one. The greater power demanded loyalty and obligated itself to the protection of the other. International treaties were conditional and depended on continued loyalties from both parties. The prophets in the Old Testament, however, saw the relationship between God and Israel as permanent, their covenant binding and everlasting. Even when the Israelites failed to live up to their God's expectations, God called them back. This willingness on God's part to enter into a new covenant is beautifully expressed in Jeremiah 31:27–37, where God puts the law within the hearts of the houses of Israel and Judah. They are forgiven, and their sins are remembered no more. In this passage, the covenantal formula is reiterated: "I will be their God, and they shall be my people" (Jer. 31:33). This formula lies at the heart of covenant keeping. I am yours. You are mine.

Throughout the centuries, as the Israelite story is remembered and retold, there is a strong and pervasive recognition that the people of Yahweh have not always been faithful to their covenant promises. Kings have been loyal; kings have been disloyal. The populace has been faithful, and they have been unfaithful. The story is one of turning away and then being called back into the relationship again. But in a post-Holocaust world, the questions about covenant and the people of Israel take a disturbing twist as one thinks about the loyalty of God. When one looks at the annihilation of six million Jews between 1939 and 1945, questions seem inevitable: Where was God? Was God true to the covenant God made with the Israelites as they as a nation were given birth? Is God a capricious God? uncaring? disloyal to the covenantal promise—I am your God and you are my people? Why was God silent at such a time as this?

(Pronounce "b'rah-chah")

Blessing

Jacob stands by the edge of the river. And he is alone. Already the stage is set in Genesis 32 for an adventure. What will happen to this man who in his youth deceived his aging blind father and tricked him into giving him the family's birthright? What will happen to this man who then traveled to the north and through scheming and deception amassed a large fortune? And what will happen to him now as he prepares to be reunited with his brother again? Will he lose his life? He sends family and friends ahead to prepare the way, perhaps to "soften" brother Esau so that their meeting will not be violent or fatal. We wonder, and Jacob wonders, and he sends his wives and maids and eleven children to the other side of the river, and he is alone. And it is night.

A man wrestles him. What man? Who is the man? Is this God? an angel or messenger? a thief? a stranger? They wrestle. It is not unlike our wrestling in the night with fears and regrets, with conscience. And when the man sees that he cannot prevail against Jacob, he strikes him on the hip socket, putting it out of joint. "Let me go," the stranger says, "day is dawning." And Jacob replies, "I will not let you go until you bless me" (Gen. 32:26, author's translation).

What is it that Jacob wants from this stranger? What does it mean to be blessed?

We wonder if, as Jacob prepares to face the brother who has vowed to kill him (Gen. 27:41), the blessing might have something to do with Jacob's life. He no longer can rely on his own wits and resources. He prays all the night long, becoming the father of his people. What is it he fights so persistently for?

The root word *berek* in Hebrew is also the word for "knee." The reason for this is not clear; perhaps at some time there was a relationship between receiving a blessing and kneeling. "Blessed be…"One does not speak this blessing to just anyone and certainly not to strangers. This blessing is given only to those to whom one is indebted or with whom one is connected socially or by the same faith. When Yahweh uses the phrase "Blessed be my people" with reference to Egypt and Assyria in Isaiah 19:25, Yahweh is saying that one day his intimate relationships with humanity given through the covenant will also be extended to Assyria and Egypt. They will be acknowledged as Yahweh's people.

Early in the life of the Hebrew people this shortened formula (Blessed be…), which implied a special relationship with a kinsperson or fellow believer, seems to have been pushed into the background, so that the one speaking the blessing did not name the one being blessed directly. The one speaking simply designated the God they both worshiped as the one being blessed. "Blessed be Yahweh, the God of _____." Have you ever wondered why in the psalms it often reads, "Blessed be Yahweh"? Does Yahweh need to be blessed?

Often, *b'rachah* in the Old Testament is transmitted from the "greater" to the "lesser," as from parent to child, or brother to sister, or king to subject. The blessing might be conveyed when one is leaving on a journey or on a special occasion. Its major function seems to have been to confer abundant and effective life. The acknowledged relationship between blessing and cursing with life and death in Deuteronomy 30:19 and elsewhere reaches at the heart of the Old Testament's understanding of blessing. God demonstrates from Genesis 12 on that God alone has power to bestow blessing. God gives life.

Perhaps this was, then, Jacob's longing by the riverside—a longing for continued life. And he received it. In the Old Testament the blessing is often set within a web of name giving and covenant making. This gives new identity and opens up a new perspective on life. Sarah, for instance, is given a new name when she shares in the blessing. In Genesis 32, Jacob is given the name "Israel." He continues to be Jacob, of course, with all that implies. He is still the trickster, schemer, and the supplanter of his elder brother. And he limps away from the riverside. He is blessed, but he limps. There is no magic blessing that eliminates reality. The once devious Jacob was not transformed overnight. Even when we are blessed by God, our humanness remains a part of us.[1]

(Pronounce "goh-el")

Redeemer

Generations have been intrigued by the story of Naomi and her two daughters-in-law, Orpah and Ruth. Faced with the devastating realities of loss and famine, they begin to forge their way into the world, taking risks and pledging support for and solidarity with one another. At the crossroads, Ruth, a Moabite, makes the decision not to return to her homeland but to travel to Bethlehem with her mother-in-law, now without husband, son, or grandchild. The pleasant one, Naomi, has become bitter. Empty. She thought Yahweh had brought calamity upon her, but she was to find that she had not been forsaken.

This is a story about redemption. In Israelite society, a man's nearest relative (brother, uncle, cousin, or another kinsman) was responsible for standing up for him and maintaining his rights. There was a strong sense of tribal solidarity. Members of the clan and their possessions held a certain kind of unity, and disruptions in the unity were intolerable and had to be restored. In this story, Boaz is the *go'el*. There is a closer relative to Elimelech, Naomi's deceased husband. But he is not willing to buy back the property for Naomi and marry her daughter-in-law. Boaz, next in line, is willing.

The redeemer had other responsibilities. If an Israelite sold himself to a foreigner as a slave, the redeemer could buy him back or redeem him. If someone was murdered, the death could be avenged by the redeemer, who would kill the murderer or a member of the killer's clan. A redeemer could also be one who would appear as a "helper" in a lawsuit to see that justice was done. A redeemer cared about the family member's rights and honor.

In the story of Ruth, then, there is a redeemer who is a close relative of Naomi's deceased husband. He is willing to buy back property. However, he is not willing to marry Naomi's daughter-in-law, which is evidently part of the bargain. But Boaz is the willing redeemer. He buys back the field for the family and marries Ruth, and together they provide Naomi with a grandson and, consequently, renewed standing in the community.

Although it is not clear how these "secular" under-standings of redeemer and redemption have influenced the theological understandings of redemption in the Old Testament, this much is clear: Yahweh performs a similar role when Yahweh is described as the "redeemer" of the fatherless and the widowed and pleads their cause (Prov. 23:11). Yahweh takes up the cause of a worshiper and redeems his life (Lam. 3:58). In the Old Testament, people are redeemed from the following:

- evil
- violence
- oppression
- the hand of the enemy
- distress
- dangers in travel
- imprisonment
- illness
- death
- sin

In Exodus, God promises to bring the people out from under the burden of the Egyptians, to redeem them with outstretched arm. The people are redeemed from slavery. Redemption, then, has something to do with being delivered, being drawn out from one world into another, being saved from that which oppresses, confines, frightens, or destroys.

And so Yahweh is labeled a redeemer. Yahweh is the one who is capable of drawing us out from one world into another, from the world of sin into one of forgiveness, from fear to courage, from oppression to a resistant voice that challenges that oppression.

> The people of Israel are oppressed, and so too are the people of Judah; all their captors have held them fast and refuse to let them go. Their Redeemer is strong; the LORD of hosts is his name. [The Lord] will surely plead their cause. (Jer. 50:33–34)

> You have taken up my cause, O Lord, you have redeemed my life. (Lam 3:58)

These and many other affirmations in the Old Testament come from people who were delivered by Yahweh from that which overwhelmed them. There are words in the psalms pleading for Yahweh to redeem. In Psalm 69 the worshiper cries out to God because the enemies are all around; more in number than the hairs on the psalmist's head are those who hate the psalmist, who pours out despair to Yahweh and implores Yahweh to help: "Answer me, O LORD, for you steadfast love is good; according to your abundant mercy, turn to me. Do not hide your face from your servant, for I am in distress–make haste to answer me. Draw near to me, redeem me" (Ps. 69:16–18).

There is an assurance in these psalms that Yahweh is able to deliver and that Yahweh will. Often, the question is, When? When will this deliverance take place? That was a question with which the rabbis wrestled, knowing out of their own life experience that deliverance, redemption, is often something for which one must wait. A rabbi once said that redemption is compared to four things: harvesting, vintaging, the gathering of spices, and a woman with child. It is compared to harvesting because when a field is harvested prematurely, even the straw is unusable. If the field is harvested at the proper time, the straw is fully usable. If the vineyard is harvested too soon, the vinegar from it is not good. If spices are gathered before they are ready, they are soft and moist and do not give off a fragrance. If a woman gives birth before her time, the child will not live.[1]

Redemption must come in its own time.

(Pronounce "gehr")

Stranger

I was celebrant at the communion of a very large gathering just a few years ago when I spoke words about the idea of being "welcome." I talked about how that word is etched deeply into the altar and that the word *welcome* is integral to and deeply embedded in our worship practice and theologies. When the service was over, a woman came up to see me. She said, "I have been estranged from the church for many years and have not felt welcomed inside its doors. Tonight for the first time in a very long time I felt welcomed to participate. But communion—the bread and the wine—wasn't offered to those of us sitting in the balcony, and once again I leave disillusioned. I wasn't really welcomed after all." And she turned and walked out into the night. I have not seen her again. I knew that she had not been intentionally left out of the ritual, and I also understood why intentionality didn't matter to her. She had a strong need to feel welcomed, to feel as if she belonged. I left troubled. The brief "conversation" I had with her sparked again what I have all my life known—that while hospitality is not commonly thought of as a theological category, it is an important and essential part of our living. How do we treat and welcome the stranger?

I actually thought I knew something about hospitality until I had the opportunity to visit Fiji, an island in the South Pacific. Attending a meeting of theological educators from the South Pacific and around the world, I couldn't have imagined the welcome they gave me—an intergenerational welcoming ceremony replete with beautiful native song and dance. Food. Drink. Gifts were given by people who do not enjoy the surplus of wealth that I enjoy. Words of blessing were spoken with a graciousness that remains unsurpassed in my memory. I came back saddened by my own lack of sensitivity to the strangers among us. What is hospitality, and how are we to treat the stranger? The Old Testament provides for us here a healthy and stirring challenge.

"You shall not oppress a stranger, you know the heart of a stranger, for you were strangers in the land of Egypt" (Ex. 23:9, author's translation). This law from the book of Exodus speaks to the heart of hospitality. Because the Israelites knew what it was like to live in another land and what it was like to be oppressed there, they were never to let those memories escape them. And in remembering, they were never to treat the stranger as they were treated in Egypt. It is not difficult for us, I suspect, to think of the times that we were the "stranger," new to the city, the country, the church. We can perhaps remember times when the language and customs of those around us were unfamiliar, when we could not understand, when life seemed risky or hard or lonely. Out of the memories of these experiences, hospitality is born.

The best translation for the Hebrew word *ger* is perhaps "resident alien." In the Old Testament, these were a special class of citizens, those who were from another place but who sojourned in the land and for a while dwelt there. The laws protecting them in the Old Testament challenge us to rethink our understandings of how our faith commitments call on us to welcome these.

Laws in Leviticus speak to the kindnesses that are to be granted to the stranger.

> You shall not strip your vineyard bare, or gather the fallen grapes of your vineyard; you shall leave them for the poor and [the stranger]: I am the LORD your God. (Lev. 19:10)

> When a stranger resides with you in your land, you shall not oppress the stranger. The stranger who resides with you shall be to you as the citizen among you; you shall love the stranger as yourself, for you were strangers in the land of Egypt. I am the LORD your God. (Lev 19:33–34, author's translation)

Several Old Testament characters are known for their hospitality. Job, perhaps because of what is written in Job 31:32 ("The stranger has not lodged in the street; I have opened my doors to the traveler"), is known for his kindness to travelers passing by. The rabbis say this about him: Job had four doors to his house—one on the north, one on the south, one on the east, and one on the west. He did this in order that the poor should not be put to the distress of having to go around the entire house; the one who came from the north could enter directly, and so forth. When the great calamity befell Job, he pleaded with the Holy One, "Master of the universe, did I not feed the hungry, give drink to the thirsty, and clothe the naked?" The Holy One answered Job, "Job, you have not yet reached half the measure of hospitality extended by Abraham. You sat in your house waiting for guests to come to you. But Abraham did not. He went out, into the world. When he met prospective guests, he brought them to his home. Not only that, but he got busy and built spacious mansions along the highways, and stocked them with food and drink, so that whoever entered ate, drank, and blessed heaven."[1]

Other stories describe Abraham as one accustomed to offering hospitality to many whom he met when he himself was a sojourner. After travelers (whom he had made his guests) had eaten and drunk, they stood up to bless him. He said to them: "Was it of mine that you ate? You ate of that which belongs to the everlasting God of the world. Thank, praise, and bless Him who spoke and the world came into being."[2] Abraham gave thanks to God, who gave him all that he had to offer the other.

That's the point. We are gracious because God has been gracious. We are welcoming because God is welcoming. We are kind to the stranger because we have ourselves been strangers.

(Pronounce "goh-lah")

Exile

One of the formative events of the Old Testament is the exile. In 586 B.C.E., the Babylonians invaded the southern kingdom of Judah and destroyed Jerusalem, the site of the temple. Many of the Jewish leaders were taken into exile and deported to Babylon. One of the ways empires in ancient times managed to control other nations was by taking the leadership of the invaded nation and transporting them to another land. To "exile" people has been one of the powerful ploys of oppressing nations throughout the ages. The history and making of America has its roots in the deportation and importation of people. Native Americans were driven from their land by immigrants from Europe and Russia and over time exiled to smaller areas of land, the reservations. The Dutch, the British, and other European countries deported a horrific number of African people, exporting them to America.

In the Old Testament, the Jews who were deported lost their connection to their land, to their place within the larger community, and to their places of worship. No doubt the deportation was partial, affecting most priests, officials, and landed citizens. And most likely the Jewish communities that were dispersed into settlements did not suffer grave injustices at the hands of their oppressors. Actually, there is some evidence to suggest that some of the exiles prospered in the new land in ways not open to them in the old. But still, land was lost. *The* land was lost, the land that had given rise to the stories of their ancestors of faith. The land of their traditions. The land of their ritual. The Israelites knew God was present with them in the temple in Jerusalem. With the destruction of the temple, the place of exile became a place without God, and their laments rose up. "Have you forgotten us completely? Why have you forsaken us?" Exile is geographical. It is also social, moral, and cultural. It has to do with the loss of home and the intense longing for it. Thus, it is a powerful theological image in late Old Testament hymnody and narrative.

The word *golah* means "exile" or "captivity." (Interestingly it also means "to uncover.") It captures this experience of the Jewish community that is ripped from its land and taken away from all it has held dear. While it is not likely that many who were deported wrote about this experience as it was happening to them, those who followed offered their own interpretations and reactions to this catastrophic event that had befallen a people. Some turned to the religion of the conquerors, assuming that the gods of the oppressor must be stronger than their own. Some were repentant, assuming that this was God's punishment for their wrongdoings. Those who were repentant often offered a word of hope that God would deliver those who had turned back. After all, their God, Yahweh, was one who delivered people from oppression. They held those ancient stories in their hearts. However the event was interpreted, it is clear that the orderly world of the exiles had fallen apart. It was a "rupture" in the whole communal fabric.

Psalm 137 gives voice to the intensity of the hurt of the Jewish community:

> On the willows there
>> we hung up our harps.
> For there our captors
>> asked us for songs,
> and our tormentors asked for mirth, saying,
>> "Sing us one of the songs of Zion!"
> How could we sing the LORD's song
>> in a foreign land?
> If I forget you, O Jerusalem,
>> let my right hand wither!
> Let my tongue cling to the roof of my mouth,
>> if I do not remember you,
> if I do not set Jerusalem
>> above my highest joy.
> Remember, O LORD, against the Edomites
>> the day of Jerusalem's fall,
> how they said, "Tear it down! Tear it down!
>> Down to its foundations!"
> O daughter Babylon, you devastator!
>> Happy shall they be who pay you back
>> what you have done to us!
> Happy shall they be who take your little ones
>> and dash them against the rock! (Ps. 137:2–9)

Exile may be a difficult concept for many to understand, those born under stable governments and never driven out of their homeland. It is a common experience, however, in several countries, where many live under continuous threat of foreign invasion and occupation. There are those who have a sense of place and belonging and those who do not. It is no wonder that contemporary readers of this psalm, those who have lost a sense of place and belonging, embrace it and see in it their own despair at having been "exiled" from their land, their homes, their churches, or the society in which they live. Exile is the loss of place, certitude, and language and the experience of being cast out into an unfamiliar world where one has to make her or his own way. This experience of exile, then, is the experience of everyone in our world who feels the loss of a guiding tradition and who has no place to rest. Everything has changed and continues to change. You cannot go home; that place no longer exists.

Theologian Ada Maria Isasi-Diaz writes about her experience and the pain of being away from her own country of Cuba against her will. She lives apart from her family and her community. The longer she is away, she says, she lives with anguish that she might someday forget her country. She recounts the time while living in California when she discovered Psalm 137, an Israelite lament, and how it gave words and identified her experience as a female and as a minority in this country. She says that praying with this psalm is cathartic; it helps her deal with the ongoing longing she has for homecoming.

As we generalize this author's experience, we realize that any in the world who experience injustice and oppression are experiencing some kind of exile, some kind of alienation from the mainstream or from whatever is life-giving and fulfilling.[1]

To be an exile from one's country, an exile within one's country, or a spiritual exile from the church is devastating. For these reasons, the rabbis, as they thought about the story in the Hebrew Bible of exile said, "Heavy is the burden of exile. It outweighs all other afflictions."[2] And another said, "There are four things the Holy One regrets having created, and one of them is exile."[3]

(Pronounce "da-bar")

Word

It is interesting to talk about the word *word*. So many contemporary sayings lead us to diminish its importance. "He's just words." "Silence is golden." "Sticks and stones will break my bones, but words..." All these lead us to the understanding that a word is not desired, is unimportant, or lacks the power to effect change. But the word *dabar* in the Old Testament is different. It is used at least 1,440 times and is the tenth most common noun.

The word *word* is an important theological term, especially in the phrase "the word of Yahweh." This is found 242 times and almost always refers to the revelation that is given to a prophet by God. The "word" comes to Isaiah (2:1), Jeremiah (1:4), Ezekiel (1:3), Hosea (1:1), Joel (1:1), Amos (3:1), Jonah (1:1), Micah (1:1), Zephaniah (1:1), Haggai (1:1), and Zechariah (1:1). Notice that notification that the words about to be heard or spoken come from Yahweh appears very early in the prophetic books, often in the very first verse. The notification that what has been spoken and ultimately written is from Yahweh serves to lend authority to the words that are spoken and to the speaker. These are the spokespersons; these are the messengers of God. Throughout the prophetic books, then, the reader is reminded by the prophet again and again that these words are not his own. These words are from God. "Thus says the Lord" is the constant refrain.

While a related term, *name*, refers to God as a person and concerns God's totality, *word* is an expression of the thoughts and will of God. *Name* mediates God's presence, but *word* symbolizes God's activity. Thus, in the Old Testament the word *word* is seen as something desired, important, and definitely having the power to bring about change.

Jeremiah gives us some very provocative imagery related to the word of God. God is railing in chapter 23 against those prophets who are speaking their own word, not God's word. These prophets are lying. They are deceitful. They are speaking to the people about their own dream. "Let the one who has my word speak my word faithfully," God says. "Is not my word like fire, says the LORD, and like a hammer that breaks a rock in pieces?" (23:28, 29). In Jeremiah, we get a sense of the sheer, brute power of God's word when it is faithful and true to God's purposes. Like fire. Like a hammer.

In Isaiah, different images come into play. God's word is like the rain and snow that come down from heaven, that water the earth, that enable it to bring forth seed for the sower and ultimately bread for the one who eats it. "So shall my word be that goes out from my mouth; it shall not return to me empty, but it shall accomplish that which I purpose, and succeed in the thing for which I sent it" (Isa. 55:11). God's word causes new life to sprout. It is right (Ps. 33:4); it is a lamp unto the feet and a light unto the path (Ps. 119:105); and it is true (119:160).

It is interesting to read Psalm 119 with an eye toward the many different names given to the expectations Yahweh has for the people. Law, decrees, commandments, statutes, precepts, ordinances, and ways—these words are repeated time and time again in the psalm's 176 verses! Of interest here are the twenty-one uses of *dabar* (vv. 9, 16, 17, 25, 42, 43, 49, 57, 65, 74, 81, 89, 101, 105, 107, 130, 139, 147, 160, 161, 169). Young people can keep their way "pure" by guarding it according to God's word. The psalmist promises never to forget it. The word is to be lived and observed. It revives us and it can be trusted. It is true. The word brings hope and comfort in times of distress. To "keep the word" is the promise of the faithful one. The word is "firmly fixed in heaven," and it is sweet to the taste, sweeter even than honey. It is a lamp and a light; it gives life and understanding.

In our own time, the Old and New Testaments have come to be known as "God's Word," though that idea is foreign to the writers of the Old Testament. It does beg the question,

Where do *we* find a word from God? in the Bible? in other places? Where do we find what refreshes, challenges, and instructs us in God's ways? What lights our path? Where do we find understanding that is sweet and delights us?

(Pronounce "da-mam")

Silence

Silence is a universal language. It is the language of the wise, the disheartened, the stunned, the grateful, the prayerful, and those who wait in hope. It is surprising, then, that this word for silence isn't more common in Old Testament literature. It is found only twenty-four times in the Old Testament canon.

There are times in the psalms when the follower of Yahweh is invited to be silent. "When you are disturbed, do not sin; ponder it on your beds, and be silent" (Ps. 4:4). Here, being silent is related to repentance and confession. Wrongdoing is often more "known" in the silence than in the noise of the everyday world. "Be silent before Yahweh, and wait patiently for God; do not fret over those who prosper in their way" (Ps. 37:7, author's translation). It is in the silence that the presence of God is made known, understanding comes, and hope is kindled.

In talking about this kind of silence, one rabbi said that three things were fitting for the Jewish community: upright kneeling, silent screaming, and motionless dance. "What does this mean?" he was asked. And he said, "Even when a Jew is standing upright, the heart must be prostrated in reverence before God. Everything in life must engender a feeling of God's presence...In adversity, and in sorrow, when a scream of despair would issue forth from the throat, man must be silent and trust in the righteousness, wisdom, and justice of God...And even when a Jew remains motionless, his soul must dance in joy before the wonder and glory of God."[1]

Perhaps one of the most well-known passages in the book of 1 Kings is the story about the prophet Elijah, making his way through the wilderness while being afraid that his life might be taken by the angry queen, Jezebel. Alone, he sleeps under a solitary tree and is awakened by a messenger who tells him to get up and eat. Miraculously, water and cake have been provided for him. After eating a second time, he travels forty days and nights to Horeb, the mount of God. He spends the night in a cave, and the word of Yahweh comes to him asking him why he is there. Elijah tells Yahweh that he is the only faithful prophet and that others are seeking his life. Yahweh says to him,

> "Go out and stand on the mountain before the LORD, for the LORD is about to pass by." Now there was a great wind, so strong that it was splitting mountains and breaking rocks in pieces before the LORD, but the LORD was not in the wind; and after the wind an earthquake, but the LORD was not in the earthquake; and after the earthquake a fire, but the LORD was not in the fire; and after the fire a sound of sheer silence. (1 Kings 19:11–12)

It was the silence of Yahweh that ushered in the conversation with Elijah. In the silence, God was found. It is this kind of silence that is experienced by preachers and pastors who in meditation prepare themselves for proclamation, and it is this kind of silence that in worship prepares the worshiping community to hear the word.

Another word in the Old Testament is translated "silence." Occasionally with this word we get a sense of the absence of God being depicted through God's silence. This is not surprising, because the revelation of God is described not only as something seen (vision) but also something heard. The psalmist describes the agony of this kind of silence. "To you, O LORD, I call; my rock, do not refuse to hear me, for if you are silent to me, I shall be like those who go down to the Pit. Hear the voice of my supplication as I cry to you for help, as I lift up my hands toward your most holy sanctuary" (Ps. 28:1–2). How can we thoughtfully think about the silence of God? In *When God Is Silent*, Barbara Brown Taylor suggests that only an idol always answers. "The God who keeps silence, even when God's own flesh and blood is begging for a word, is the God beyond anyone's control. An answer will come, but not until the silence is complete. And even then, the answer will be given in silence."[2]

This word is about God's silence and human silence. In Isaiah it is used to describe both. In Third Isaiah, the prophet declares his own compulsion to speak—something akin to Jeremiah's fire in the bones. "For Zion's sake I will not keep silent, and for Jerusalem's sake I will not rest," the prophet says (Isa. 62:1). The prophet has a message for all nations about the vindication for Yahweh's people who are now given a new name and are the Lord's delight. Sentinels are posted on the walls of Jerusalem, and they "shall never be silent" (62:6). Their job is to remind Yahweh continually to take no rest until Jerusalem is reestablished and finds her rightful and renowned place. The prophet calls upon Yahweh not to be silent (64:12). The prophet knows, however, that when Yahweh chooses to speak, it is not what the community wants to hear. "I will not keep silent, but I will repay; I will indeed repay into their laps their iniquities and their ancestors' iniquities together…because they offered incense on the mountains and reviled me on the hills" (65:6–7). When the people are not faithful to the covenant, Yahweh cannot keep silent about the betrayal.

Whatever this silence means, there is a time for it. The author of Ecclesiastes 3, in talking about the seasons of our lives, reminds us that there is a time for all of heaven's matters. A time to be born and to die, to plant and to pluck up, to kill and to heal, to break down and to build up, to weep and to laugh, to mourn and to dance, to throw away stones and to gather stones, to embrace and to refrain from embracing, to seek and to lose, to keep and to throw away, to tear and to sew, to love and to hate, to make war and to have peace. There is also a time to speak and a time to keep silence.

A Jewish legend tells the story of a peddler who went around to villages selling his wares, crying, "Who'd like the elixir of life?" Everybody gathered around and said to him, "Give us the elixir of life." While seated in his reception chamber, a rabbi heard the peddler crying, "Who'd like the elixir of life?" He called out, "Come up here and sell it to me!" The peddler said, "Not to you nor to the likes of you." But the rabbi insisted, so the peddler came up to him, took out a book of Psalms, and showed him the verse, "Which of you desires life?...Keep your tongue from evil" (Ps. 34:12–13).The rabbi said, "All the days I have been reading this verse, but I did not realize its plain meaning until this peddler came by and made me aware of it."[3] The rabbi had learned that there were times when it was best to keep silence. So many of the proverbs teach us this same truth. Wisdom comes from knowing when to speak, when not to speak, what to speak, and what not to speak. It is about knowing the value of word *and* silence.

(Pronounce "zah-car")

To Remember

Most children love the story of Noah and the ark. In Sunday school they draw pictures of the big boat riding rough waves of the stormy sea. Always there are two very long-necked giraffes peering out from the boat's topside. The story entices our imaginations and our fantasies. What's not to love?

Years later, of course, we realize that the story was forged in the shocking realities of life, and it gives birth to a few very thorny theological questions about God. It is a story, after all, about a God who looks on all of creation and with sadness and despair decides that how they have chosen to live life cannot be tolerated. It is the violence that God cannot bear to see. God says, "Enough!" And God decides to wipe out creation with a rainstorm that lasts forty days and nights. The person telling us this story says that the people had evil imaginations in their hearts. This understanding of the world is not totally foreign to our own—a world divided, a world of fear and mistrust, a world where difference some-times means death. It is not the world God envisioned or hoped for. The evil hearts of women and men grieve God's own.

The flood comes, and only those on the ark are saved. Noah and his family take a step off the boat, and life begins again. Very quickly we realize that the world is going to be the same, that people will continue to abuse and use and degrade one another. And we wonder, Has anything or anyone changed? The answer is yes. God has. God sits back and looks at the world created, gone astray, now destroyed, and beginning again. And with a deep grief, God says, "Never again. Never again will there be a flood to destroy the earth. I'll put a sign up in the sky, a bow in the clouds. I will put it there so that I can remember the covenant that I am making with my people...I am your God. You are my people. This is the way we must live together. I am yours, and you are mine. I will put the bow in the sky and I will remember this covenant I have with every living person and every living creature on the face of the earth. Whenever I see the bow in the cloud, I will remember" (see Gen. 9:11–16).

The verb "to remember" is an important one in the Old Testament. When God remembers the covenant as God has promised to do, acts of redemption take place. God delivers the people from bondage (Ex. 2:24), and God preserves them as they travel throughout the wilderness (Lev. 26:44–45). For God not to remember the iniquity of the people is to forgive them and to withhold further judgment (Ps. 79:8–9). So it is that remembering is not just recalling a memory, but it is a recalling that culminates in some kind of activity. Memorials designed to help us remember something or someone are purposeful not because they bring the event or person to mind, but because in remembering we are prompted to act in certain ways. Thus, in the psalms, lamenters often call to and ask God to remember them or remember something about them (Ps. 89:47; see also 25:6, 7; 74:2; 106:4).

People are also called to remember, of course. "O give thanks to the LORD, call on [God's] name, make known [remember] [God's] deeds among the peoples. Sing to [God], sing praises to [God], tell of [God's] wonderful works" (Ps. 105:1–2). This psalm and others go on to tell the story of God's deeds in relation to the community of Israel. The community is asked to remember that God made a covenant with their ancestors, delivered the people from Egypt by sending Moses to lead them, and brought them into the land. The details of the journey and the persons who led them along the way are recited as reminders of the many ways God has been with them in the past. In Psalm 105, to remember is not just for remembering's sake. The story is to be remembered so that thanksgiving can be given to the God who has led them and so that the story can be told to others.

(Pronounce "cheht")

Sin

In Judges 20:15–16, the storyteller reports that the Benjaminites went out to battle, twenty-six thousand of them armed for warfare. Seven hundred of these were left-handed; every one of them could sling a stone at a hair and not "miss." In a different way, Proverbs 19:2 talks about one who moves too hurriedly and "misses the way." The woman or man gets lost. In Proverbs 8, wisdom herself speaks and says that the one who listens to her is happy: "Whoever finds me finds life and obtains favor from the LORD; but those who miss me injure themselves; all who hate me love death" (Prov. 8:35–36). In all these instances the verb "miss" or "misses the way" is *chata'*, the same word that is translated "to sin." We can learn from this that sin must have something to do with missing the mark, akin to a soldier missing a target, or a traveler going in the wrong direction, or a person not being able to find what is good and right. These are all definitions of sin in the Old Testament—missing the goal or standard God has set for us, trying and not succeeding, or traveling down the wrong path.

Different parts and kinds of literature in the Old Testament fill in the picture for us. We are reminded of the many ways that people frequently miss the mark or lose their way. We are also reminded in Proverbs that these sins have consequences.

If the righteous are repaid on earth, how much more the wicked and the sinner! (Prov. 11:31)

In the Psalms, the lamenter is often confessing personal or community sins:

O, LORD, be gracious to me;
heal me, for I have sinned against you. (Ps. 41:4)

Against you, you alone, have I sinned, and done what is evil in your sight, so that you are justified in your sentence and blameless when you pass judgment. Indeed, I was born guilty, a sinner when my mother conceived me. (51:4–5)

Both we and our ancestors have sinned;
we have committed iniquity, have done wickedly. (106:6)

And in the books of the prophets, the spokespersons for God name the community's sin. See particularly the writings of Jeremiah, who names clearly the people's condition (Jer. 3:25; 8:14; 14:7, 20; 16:10).

The rabbis were aware of the tenacity of our sinful natures. "All of man's iniquities are engraved upon his bones," they said.[1] "A man's impulse to evil renews itself everyday."[2] They believed that surely the inclination to commit sin must be older than that to do good, so pervasive it is. The rabbis said: "The impulse to evil is at least thirteen years older than the impulse to good. Only at the age of thirteen is the impulse to good born in a child."[3]

The rabbis also said, "When a man stirs up his passion and is about to commit an act of lewdness, all parts of his body are ready to obey him. On the other hand, when man is about to perform an act of piety, all his parts become laggard, because the impulse to evil in his innards is ruler of the two hundred and forty-eight parts of his body, whereas the impulse to good is like a man confined to a prison."[4]

Sin, then, is that which is opposed to God's purposes for the created order. Sins are committed against God, God's laws, God's creation, God's covenant and purpose.

Although sin in the Old Testament was seen as inevitable and universal, the rabbis knew that life would be better without it! "Happy is the man who at the time of his death is as free of sin as at the time of his birth."[5]

(Pronounce "chok-mah")

Wisdom

The book of Proverbs starts with an announcement that the short wisdom sayings it contains come from Solomon, the son of David, king of Israel. In this book and in the narratives about Solomon in the book of Kings, Solomon is known for this extraordinary wisdom, which he exhibits as he makes the important decisions inherent in leadership. The book begins with a brief introduction about wisdom, asserting that "the fear of the LORD is the beginning of knowledge; fools despise wisdom and instruction" (Prov. 1:7). The stage is set, then, and the invitation securely in place. Those who seek wisdom will read further. Fools will not.

Immediately then, a child is addressed and given his parent's instruction. The words are eerily familiar to any parent who wants a child to make good and right decisions: "If sinners entice you, do not consent" (1:10). And there you have it. Parents want children to stay away from anyone who would lead them astray. They want a child to know that evil ones are lying in wait. They do not want the child to be easily persuaded or to be naive.

Then she appears, first in simple brush strokes that tell us little about her. We wonder who she is; we know only that her name is Wisdom. She cries out in the street and raises her voice on the noisiest of street corners. She has called out before, but the world has not listened to her. And so she calls out again.

The scene suddenly changes, and the child is addressed again. "My child, if you accept my words and treasure up my commandments within you, making your ear attentive to wisdom and inclining your heart to understanding…if you seek it like silver…then you will understand the fear of the LORD and find the knowledge of God" (2:1–5). Yes, spoken like a parent. "My child" is again addressed in chapter 3, in verse 1 and then again in verse 11. (See also 3:21; 4:1, 10, 20; 5:1, 7, 20; 6:1, 3, 20; 7:1, 24; 8:32.) The parent is insistent and hopes intensely that the child will listen.

Then female Wisdom appears again. A few more brush strokes of her portrait are put into place. She is more precious than jewels, and nothing that can be desired can compare with her (3:15). She holds the keys to long life and peace; she is the tree of life and the source of happiness (vv. 16–18). It is by wisdom that the LORD founded the earth (v. 19). She can keep, guard, and love (4:6). She is to be prized (v. 8). She can be found on the heights, beside the way, at the crossroads, and beside the gates of the city (8:2–3). She can be found anywhere.

Then the portrait of Wisdom comes to us in its fullness.

The LORD created me at the beginning of his work, the first of his acts of long ago. Ages ago I was set up, at the first, before the beginning of the earth. When there were no depths I was brought forth, when there were no springs abounding with water...When he established the heavens, I was there...when he marked out the foundations of the earth, then I was beside him, like a master worker; and I was daily his delight, rejoicing before him always, rejoicing in his inhabited world and delighting in the human race. (8:22–31)

The rabbis said, "The spirit conceived and gave birth to wisdom."[1]

Who is this female Wisdom? It is no surprise that throughout the centuries this female figure has captured and intrigued the imaginations of biblical scholars. Does this female symbolize an attribute of God? Is she a separate entity from God? Is she like many of the female goddesses of the other religions in the Ancient Near East?

This personification of wisdom and the scores and scores of sayings that are listed in other portions of the book of Proverbs are unlike other material in the Old Testament in that there is not recounted here the histories or remembrances of the long history Yahweh has had with the people. There is no mention of the patriarchs and matriarchs, or the exodus, or the conquest. Yahweh's great deeds are not celebrated, nor are people reminded that they are part of a covenantal history. This book is about experience, lived experience. With short, pithy sayings that are usually written in two lines parallel to each other, sometimes paradoxical and always drawn from keen observations about life, the proverbs reflect our experiences back to us. They are about wisdom and where it can be found. Proverbs describes for us what a wise life looks like in its living—the ethics of work, of family life, and of friendship.

When pride comes, then comes disgrace; but wisdom is with the humble. (11:2)

How much better to get wisdom than gold! To get understanding is to be chosen rather than silver. (16:16)

The fear of the LORD is instruction in wisdom, and humility goes before honor. (15:33)

Wisdom comes from fearing Yahweh. Wisdom is precious. It comes from humility, a willingness to listen to the advice of others and to seek counsel. It manifests itself in how we go about our living and our treating of others. A rabbi said, "Who is wise? He who learns from everyone, as is said. Because everyone has been my teacher, I have gained understanding."[2]

So what does wisdom teach us? A trip through the very long lists in Proverbs (in chapters 10—29) proves an interesting journey, sometimes an entertaining one, but always an enlightening one. Following are a few of them: The mouths of fools are their ruin, and their lips a snare to themselves (18:7). One who is slack in work is close kin to a vandal (18:9). The human spirit will endure sickness, but a broken spirit—who can bear? (18:14). Many seek the favor of the generous, and everyone is a friend to a giver of gifts (19:6). Laziness brings on deep sleep; an idle person will suffer hunger (19:15). Hatred stirs up strife, but love covers all offenses (10:12). Like vinegar to the teeth, and smoke to the eyes, so are the lazy to their employers (10:26). Whoever belittles another lacks sense, but an intelligent person remains silent (11:12). Anxiety weighs down the human heart, but a good word cheers it up (12:25). Even in laughter the heart is sad, and the end of joy is grief (14:13). A soft answer turns away wrath, but a harsh word stirs up anger (15:1). Better is a dinner of vegetables where love is than a fatted ox and hatred with it (15:17). Pleasant words are like a honeycomb, sweetness to the soul and health to the body (16:24). Sometimes there is a way that seems to be right, but in the end it is the way to death (16:25). Gray hair is a crown of glory; it is gained in a righteous life (16:31). Better is a dry morsel with quiet than a house full of feasting with strife (17:1). Grandchildren are the crown of the aged, and the glory of children is their parents (17:6). A cheerful heart is a good medicine, but a downcast spirit dries up the bones (17:22). Some friends play at friendship but a true friend sticks closer than one's nearest kin (18:24).

What makes this list of proverbs or aphorisms different from any other list of proverbs—a list in the *Farmer's Almanac*, for instance? It is clear throughout the book of Proverbs that the fear of God is the beginning of wisdom. "It was perhaps her [Israel's] greatness that she did not keep faith and knowledge apart. The experiences of the world were for her always divine experiences as well, and the experiences of God were for her experiences of the world."[3] Wisdom provides a model for living. To know God is to be in and *to do* truth. Thus, the Hebrew word *derek*, or "way," is found some seventy-five times in Proverbs. There is a "way" that life is to be lived; a way that secures life in a full sense. The "way" is how each of us incarnates the teachings of the wise ones and has to do with honesty, diligence, self-control, and assuming responsibility for one's own life. Wisdom has to do with integrity and character and the folly of not having them. Thus, the proverbs describe well the motivations and temptations that are part and parcel of trying to live life out in the midst of our families and our colleagues and our neighborhoods and the world.

(Pronounce "cheh-sed")

Steadfast Love

Read through Psalm 136. This call to thanksgiving gives praise to Yahweh, for Yahweh is good. It gives thanks to the God of gods. It gives thanks to the Lord of lords. All this praise and thanksgiving flows out of the knowledge that the steadfast love, *hesed*, endures forever. The psalm then recounts the wondrous deeds of this God, the one who has created the heavens and the earth, the great lights. This is the one who brought the Israelites out of Egypt, through the Red Sea, and through the many dangers of the wilderness. The psalm closes with another affirmation of thanksgiving.

Punctuating this psalm is a phrase found twenty-six times, once in each verse. "For [God's] steadfast love endures forever." This psalm is a celebration of a love that is faithful, constant, and sure. It is the kind of love that actively seeks the well-being of the other. It is the kind of love that offers the best the world has to offer and constantly seeks redemption for the one in need.

This Hebrew word is found some 245 times in the Old Testament. It sometimes speaks of the kind of relationship found between two people, those who love and offer the best to each other. In the story of Ruth and Naomi, Naomi wishes for her daughters-in-law a good life. As the three widows stand together and prepare to say good-bye to one another, Naomi tells them to go back to their homeland, and she blesses them. "May Yahweh [do *hesed* to] you, as you have dealt with the dead and with me" (Ruth 1:8). Naomi is asking that Yahweh watch over them faithfully and steadfastly. We are overwhelmed by the devotion and commitment Ruth shows to her mother-in-law when she decides to forfeit the security and comfort of homeland to accompany Naomi back to Bethlehem. As a kinsman, Boaz watches over them and allows Ruth to glean in the fields. Naomi, who has been bitter about what life has dealt her, says, "Blessed be he by the LORD, whose kindness *has not forsaken the living or the dead!*" (2:20, emphasis author's). Through the loving and welcoming acts of Boaz, Naomi once again knows the steadfast love of the God who has not abandoned her. And in the end, Boaz names the sacrifices Ruth has made to care for her mother-in-law as this same kind of steadfast love (3:10).

Rahab, the prostitute in the city of Jericho who hid and protected the Israelites who had come to "scout" the city, is described as having *hesed*. She asks that the kindness (mercy, love) that she has shown to the Israelites be returned to her family (Josh. 2:12). In a different story, Abimelech, having taken in Abraham as a guest, asks him to show the same kind of love to his host and the land where he has sojourned (Gen. 21:23).When this kind of love is received, it is then given.

A rabbi tells of the subjects of a king who came before him and said, "Oh our King, we would show our love for thee. What shall we say unto thee? What gifts may we give thee?" The King answered, "My subjects, I am grateful for your goodness in coming before me to show your love. But what words shall you utter? I know the sentiments of your hearts. What gifts can you give? Am I not the king, the ruler of the entire realm? If you would show your love for me, attend to my words. I have children, and I cherish them dearly. If you would show your love for me, then go forth and serve my children."[1]

The angels in Genesis 19 show this kind of love in saving the life of Lot and his family. David, in facing the son of his friend Jonathan, says to him, "Do not be afraid, for I will show you *hesed* for the sake of your father Jonathan; I will restore to you all the land of your grandfather Saul, and you will be welcome at my table always" (2 Sam. 9:7, author's translation).

These and other stories in the Old Testament demonstrate how this kind of love is made manifest in human relationships. Whether shown between relatives, between nations, between strangers who have become acquaintances, or between friends, this kind of love is how communities are knit together. This kind of love has certain attributes:

- **Active.** It is not just an attitude to be possessed; it is the act that emerges from the attitude. It is an act that preserves or promotes life. It is an intervention on behalf of someone who suffers misfortune or distress. It is a demonstration of friendship or piety. It pursues what is good and not evil. Often this kind of love is paired in the Old Testament with justice. The famous quotation in Micah 6:8, for instance, makes an effort to say succinctly what God requires of us: to do justice and to love this kind of enduring love, and to walk humbly with God. Martin Luther King, Jr., put it this way: "Love that does not satisfy justice is no love at all. It is merely a sentimental affection, little more than one would have for a pet. Love at its best is justice concretized."[2]

- **Social.** It has to do with relationship. It is given and received.

- **Enduring.** Close and intimate community requires enduring and reliable kindness as an essential element of its ability to protect those who are a part of it.

Most often, however, this word is used to speak of the kind of love God has for humanity. We have often in our churches been led to believe that the Old Testament God is one of anger, judgment, and fierce expectation, while the New Testament offers the portrait of a God who loves and who offers salvation. But that is not so. This God of steadfast love (sometimes translated "mercy" or "compassion") is alive and well in Old Testament narrative and song. God gives this kind of love. God sends it, remembers it, continues it, shows it, causes it, makes it great, keeps it, satisfies it, and surrounds it. Yahweh's love is with the worshiper. God delights in it. This is the kind of love that sees us through weakness, confusion, complaint, temptation, sin, and defeat. It is the love that indwells the human spirit, inspires hope and courage, and enables us to be faithful even when we grow weary of doing good works. This kind of love is experienced in community as care—even when the other is unlovable or unwanted. This kind of love is not sentimental or easily duped. It works in relationship; that is to say, it is creative. When options appear to be limited or closed or when meaning has collapsed, steadfast love creates a way to open our experiences to new horizons of meaning and fulfillment. It is the most difficult kind of love to justify, and yet it is the love that the psalmists long for.

Wondrously show your steadfast love. (Ps. 17:7)

Surely goodness and [steadfast love] shall follow me all the days of my life. (23:6)

Let your steadfast love O LORD, be upon us. (33:22)

God will send forth his steadfast love and his faithfulness. (57:3)

Those who prayed these prayers believed in the active, enduring love God has for them. Their testimonies grow out of the histories of their people and out of their own lives. In our own communities we sing about this kind of love: "O Love That Wilt Not Let Me Go."[3]

(Pronounce "yah-reh")

Fear

"'Twas grace that taught my heart to fear, and grace my fears relieved."[1] We sing these words from the second verse of "Amazing Grace" so easily, but rarely do we consider their complexity. There is a paradox here, one that helps us clearly understand the varied uses of the word *fear* in the Old Testament. Grace taught my heart to fear. Grace relieved my fears. Can grace do both? Yes.

We first meet Shiphrah and Puah in Exodus 1; they are Hebrew midwives living in Egypt. The Israelites are slaves there, and as their population grows in number, they become a threat to the king—they need to be "dealt with." The Egyptian taskmasters deal with them even more harshly. They are ruthless and make the lives of the Israelites bitter. In a further effort to limit the strength and growth of the Israelites, and no doubt fearing a rebellion, the Egyptian king goes to these two midwives and commands them to kill every male Israelite baby. They can let the females live. But the storyteller says, "But the midwives feared God; they did not do as the king of Egypt commanded them, but they let the boys live" (Ex. 1:17).

We cannot overestimate the amount of courage it must have taken to disobey the king! But they do, and the whole remarkable story of the deliverance from Egypt now comes into being. The boy child Moses is allowed to live, and he becomes the chosen one from God who delivers the Israelites from Egypt.

The midwives "feared" God. This story brings into focus one of the meanings of the word *fear* in the Old Testament. Here, as in other places, the word is associated with right living. Because a person fears God, she makes good decisions about how to live out life. In other places in the Old Testament (see Deut. 10:18–20), when one fears God, one treats the stranger with kindness and with respect. In Job, Yahweh asks Satan to consider Job: "There is no one like him on the earth, a blameless and upright man who fears God and turns away from evil" (Job 1:8). Satan answers, "Does Job fear God for nothing?" (Job 1:9). In this story, to fear is to live blamelessly and to be a follower of God. The fearer of God in the Old Testament walks in the way of Yahweh and is blessed with happiness, goodness, provision of needs, mercy, and fulfilled desires.

Second Kings 17 brings to us another story that helps us understand that worship is a manifestation of fearing God. In the story the people "fear" God but worship other deities as well. They are reminded that they are in covenant with Yahweh and that they are not to worship other gods—only God, who brought them out of Egypt. They are reminded again that they are to "fear" Yahweh only (2 Kings 17:36, 39). The *New Revised Standard Version* of the Bible translates the word *yare'* as "worship." To fear Yahweh only is to worship Yahweh only.

The community is often described as being afraid at the sight or sound of God (see Ex. 3:6; Deut. 5:5; Isa. 6:5). The

Israelites in the wilderness were terrified at the prospect of hearing the voice of God and wanted Moses to be an intercessor for them. They hid their faces, thinking that to get a glimpse of this awesome God would mean death. To fear was to have a sense of the wild and "terrible" and awesome power of God, and this fear resulted in reverence, worship, and obedience. It is fear generated by realizing the holiness of God. Proverbs tell us that this kind of fear of God is the beginning of wisdom (Prov. 9:10).

At the same time there is consistently through our Old and New Testament texts the admonition not to fear. "Do not fear" or "Fear not" or "Do not be afraid" are words that frequently come to the lips of Old Testament characters. Sometimes they are reassuring and comforting one another. The midwife in Genesis 35:17 assures Rachel: "Do not be afraid; for now you will have another son." Jonathan uses the phrase to hearten David (1 Sam. 23:17). Sometimes the phrase is used in the context of war and battle, particularly when the war is seen as a war for Yahweh. The leader encourages the army troops to be fearless and courageous when facing the enemy. It is used by priests when they are delivering a word of comfort and salvation to a worshiper. And lastly, the phrase "Do not fear" is delivered by Yahweh as Yahweh seeks to become known either directly or through a messenger to one who is in distress. In distress one is to remember that indeed God is present (e.g., Ex. 20:20; Judg. 6:23; Dan. 10:12).

The understanding of the "fear of Yahweh" is fundamental to Old Testament theology. Eighty percent of the time that the word is used in the Old Testament, the object of fear is God. Fear of God does seemingly opposite things: It breeds terror, retreat, and flight on the one hand; attraction, love, and trust on the other. So yes, grace teaches the heart to fear. We are given chances again and again to remember that abundant life comes from fearing God—worshiping and living in right relationship to those around us. And yes, grace relieves our fears because we remember that this God also walks beside us on our journeys. We can face anything.

(Pronounce "yah-sha")

Salvation

The word *salvation* is found 354 times in the Old Testament. The largest concentration of occurrences is in the Psalms (136) and then in the prophetic books (100). It is a poetic word often found in beautiful phrases, such as the "wells of salvation" (Isa. 12:3), the "rock of our salvation" (Ps. 95:1), the "shield of your salvation"(Ps. 18:35), and the "joy of your salvation" (Ps. 51:12).[1] Whatever salvation is—it is something to sing about!

The Israelites under the leadership of Moses had left Egypt and were beginning their journey toward a land they had never seen, never known. As they begin the long and torturous journey, they set up camp between Migdol and the sea, just as Yahweh has told them. When Pharaoh finds out that the Israelites have left, he regrets having let them go. He takes the chariots and the officers over them, and they begin to the pursue the Israelites, who have made a temporary home by the sea. The Israelites look back and see the Egyptians advancing on them. They are afraid, and they cry out to the Lord. And to Moses. They are afraid that they are going to die in this place that is not home to them. "We would prefer to have died in Egypt!" they cry out. But Moses says to the people, "Do not be afraid, stand firm, and see the deliverance [salvation] that the LORD will accomplish for you today; for the Egyptians whom you see today you shall never see again. The LORD will fight for you, and you have only to keep still" (Ex. 14:13–14).

The rest of the story is one of the most well-known Old Testament narratives. Popularized by film and painting, we hold in our minds various images of Moses stretching out his hand over the sea, the waves dividing to let the Israelites pass on to freedom. At the end of the story the narrator says to us, "Thus the LORD saved Israel that day" (v. 30).

Exodus 15, which follows the recounting of this story of deliverance, preserves the words of a very old hymn. Reportedly, Moses and the Israelites, having crossed the sea, sing this song to Yahweh: "The LORD is my strength and my might, and he has become my salvation" (v. 2). It is clear from the story that God brings salvation through the parting of the waters and through the angel of God and the pillar of cloud that protect them from the enemy army. What is most interesting about the word in this context is that it is *not* usually used to describe the exodus from Egypt itself. It is used, however, to describe the deliverance through the sea.[2]

The rabbis speak about salvation this way: To what may Israel when leaving Egypt be compared? Israel can be compared to a dove who fled from a hawk and was about to enter a cleft in a rock. She came upon a serpent nesting there. If she entered the cleft, the serpent would hiss and threaten her. If she turned back, the hawk standing outside would seize her. What did she do? She began to cry and beat her wings so that the owner would come and deliver her. Israel at the Red Sea was in a similar plight. They could not go down into the sea, because the sea had not divided. Nor could they go back, because Pharaoh was drawing near. What did they do? They were afraid; and the children of Israel cried out unto the Lord. At once the Lord saved Israel that day.[3]

Salvation in the Old Testament was primarily corporate or communal and was "of this world" in character. Salvation was for the people of Israel—together. In the Wisdom literature and the Psalms, however, salvation took on a more "individual" flavor—though still it was something that happened in "this world." Nearly half the Psalms contain one or more occurrences of this word for salvation![4] Read through the cries for salvation (for both community and individual) from those who are lamenting and desperately need a response from God:

Help [Save], O LORD, for there is no longer anyone who is godly; the faithful have disappeared from humankind. (Ps. 12:1)

O save your people, and bless your heritage; be their shepherd, and carry them forever. (28:9)

Give victory [salvation] with your right hand, and answer us, so that those whom you love may be rescued. (60:5)

Give victory [salvation] with your right hand, and answer me, so that those whom you love may be rescued. (108:6)

So that I may...rejoice in your deliverance [salvation]. (9:14)

He has remembered his steadfast love and faithfulness to the house of Israel. All the ends of the earth have seen the victory [salvation] of our God. (98:3)

I hope for your salvation, O LORD. (119:166)

Just these few verses demonstrate how the psalmists cry out for God to come to them in their distress. They desire to be rescued from what brings them fear or misery or pain.

"Why are you far from saving me?" "Bring salvation from those who hate me." Thus, salvation could come time and time again when the community or individuals were delivered from their despair.

It is thought by some that the word *salvation* is related to other words meaning "spacious" and "wide."[5] There is in this notion a hopefulness that God can deliver us from what restricts us and oppresses us. We are given room, a liberating space within which we can live our lives.

This communal or individual "this world" understanding of salvation is very different from the one held by many contemporary Christians who understand the question "Are you saved?" to be of the utmost and fundamental importance. For these, salvation is a once-in-a-lifetime event; a positive response means that your soul has been saved for eternity—has been "plucked from the jaws of death."

This understanding of salvation is also different from attitudes of pessimism or cynicism. The first of these says that the human condition is fatally flawed, and whatever good measure comes is a matter of luck. The second says that nothing ever changes fundamentally for the better or for the worse. Nothing can be called "salvation." Nothing can preserve us from the contradictions, evils, madness, or sufferings of the human condition.

The Old Testament understanding of the notion of salvation holds that God actively participates in the life of the community and in the life of an individual, that God hears the cries of distress that arise from humanity, and that God is willing and desirous that we be given a full and wide berth to live out life abundantly. It stands as a correction to those theologies that understand salvation only in personal terms (evangelical Christianity) or only in communal terms (e.g., liberation theologies). The word is a testimony to God's willingness to come to us and keep coming to us as the world brings its tragedy and despair.

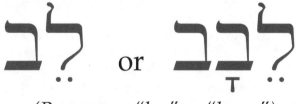

(Pronounce "lev" or "levav")

Heart

Following are some of the thoughts we often hold about "heart." "The heart of the matter" means that which is fundamental, essential, of supreme importance, and irreducible. The heart may be associated with "courage" in battle or endurance (not fainthearted). Heart is the center of the human person from which emotions and values arise.

From the heart come the issues of life. Consequently, heart may be portrayed as devious and perverse, or as pure, upright and clean, sincere and genuine. God looks on the heart, the inner person, while others may only see the surface or facade. The heart and mind stand in contrast to each other. The first is equated with emotions, mercy, and compassion. The heart has its reasons that the mind will never understand because the mind is equated with reason, logic, and power. How do these understandings coincide with Old Testament understanding of heart?

The two Hebrew words for heart listed above (which seem to be synonymous and interchangeable) are found more than 800 times in our Old Testament. The word *heart* appears in all the books of the Old Testament except Micah and Habakkuk. It is not surprising that it is found most frequently in the psalms. There are also many occurrences in Proverbs (98) and in the prophets.[1]

The Old Testament scarcely uses the word *lev* for the physical organ we know as the heart. It serves in the absence of a Hebrew word for breast or chest.[2] It can mean the area of the body around the heart. It is the fixed point, the central point, the nucleus of something, the most important part of whatever is represented. "Heart and kidneys" (Ps. 7:10) stands for the inmost nature of a person that is known only to God. "Heart and lips" (Prov. 23:16) contrasts the interior and exterior, which should be in harmony in an upright person.[3] The heart is hidden from human sight; it is deep, unsearchable. It can symbolize the essence or fundamental nature of a person.

The heart is more than the person, however; it is the most vital center of that person. It needs to be refreshed with bread. Wine rejoices the heart. People lament because they feel afflicted to the very core of their being. The heart throbs and beats wildly in anguish. The heart grows soft as wax and melts. The heart trembles, is hot as fire. It can be sick. Sin or misfortune or sickness affects the heart; it can be appalled, can break, or can even die. The heart is the seat of sexual desire.

The heart is the center of human emotion; it pounds, flutters, convulses. This symbolizes excitement, fear, and apprehension. The heart also skips with joy. The heart grieves (more often than it feels joy or pleasure!) because of childlessness, bad news, the destruction of Jerusalem, vanity, sickness, threats from the enemy, and sin. That the heart is grieving is known by one's refusal to eat, by tears, being disquiet, having a sad countenance. It weighs one down and, finally, leads to death.

The heart fears when the enemy is known to be superior, when siege and battle threaten. Fear is the reaction of the heart to rumored disaster, threats, hostility. Danger, poverty, insults, and discouragement cause the heart to despair. The heart faints, trembles, is wrung, and finally fails. The heart of the people can melt like water or shake like a tree. The heart can feel love, hate, anger, stubbornness, arrogance, courage, vice, and virtue. A heart can be wicked. If you want to comfort someone, you "speak to her heart." It is the source of gratitude for all that Yahweh has done.

In the Old Testament the heart is even more than the seat of emotion. It is the lodging place of wisdom, of what we think. It is the seat of thought and intellect and is a synonym for the mind. It is the place where decisions are made. In essence, it is the person—all that she thinks, feels, knows, and does.[4]

A listing of some of the many proverbs written about the human heart teases our minds and imaginations with questions about the way we go about our living:

Those who trust in their own wits [hearts] are fools; but those who walk in wisdom come through safely. (Prov. 28:26)

Like the glaze covering an earthen vessel are smooth lips with an evil heart. (26:23)

Like vinegar on a wound is one who sings songs to a heavy heart. (25:20)

My child, if your heart is wise, my heart too will be glad. (23:15)

Haughty eyes and a proud heart—the lamp of the wicked—are sin. (21:4)

One's own folly leads to ruin, yet the heart rages against the LORD. (19:3)

A cheerful heart is a good medicine, but a downcast spirit dries up the bones. (17:22)

The mind [heart] of the righteous ponders how to answer, but the mouth of the wicked pours out evil. (15:28)

There are six things that the LORD hates, seven that are an abomination to him: haughty eyes, a lying tongue, and hands that shed innocent blood, a heart that devises wicked plans, feet that hurry to run to evil, a lying witness who testifies falsely, and one who sows discord in a family. (6:16–19)

Do not let loyalty and faithfulness forsake you; bind them around your neck, write them on the tablet of your heart. (3:3)

The heart is these things, does all these things, knows these things. And in the Old Testament this one thing is true: It is Yahweh who knows the heart. Even before a person shapes a thought in the heart, the Holy One understands it.[5]

Theologian Howard Thurman offers us a wonderful perspective on the importance of the human heart:

Always we live under some necessity for righting our relations with our fellows. We turn to the scrutiny of the light in our hearts to see wherein we have lived without harmony, without order, and without an increasing measure of tranquility and peace. We look at the misunderstandings which we have experienced during the week that has passed. Those moments when our words conveyed what was not our intent, and the result of their movement into the life of another, brought chaos and pain and misery. Those moments when with clear-eyed intent we have gone out of our path to do the vengeful thing, to speak or to act with hardness of heart. We remember all of our reactions to the ill will in the world, to the bitterness that has loomed large between peoples and states, between countries, and between nations. All of these things weigh heavily upon our minds and spirits as we seek somehow within ourselves to be whole and clean and purified.[6]

The heart is the essence of who we are—how we think and feel and carry out our living in relationship to God and to the world.

(Pronounce "mah-yim")

Water

Water is an elemental property of nature and of the human body. In one of the creation stories of Genesis, water was there at the dawn of creation when God caused the divine spirit to move over the face of the waters. It assumes many forms—clouds, rain, rivers, lakes, oceans, snow, and ice. Because it is such an elemental property of life, it lends itself to the religious imagination, ritual, and symbolization. Every culture and religious tradition has a story or parable about water and its effects, its surface, and its depths. It is a metaphor for spirituality: "Deep River" and "Roll, Jordan,

Roll" are two examples of the way water is used in song to talk about God and God's relationship with the world. Water is essential to our living, and thus the rabbis said, "The world can live without wine, but the world cannot live without water. The world can live without pepper, but the world cannot live without salt."[1]

Psalm 104 illustrates how close the relationship is between water and the God who created and controls it. At God's rebuke the waters flee and take flight (Ps. 104:7); they rise up to the mountains and go down into the valleys (v. 8); they flow within the boundaries God sets for them (v. 9). God makes springs gush forth, giving drink to the animals and watering the earth (vv. 10–13). The trees receive water so that the birds can build nests in them (vv. 16–17). God has created the sea (v. 25).

The multifaceted dimensions and properties of water allow it to be used as a metaphor in an amazing number of ways. It is used to symbolize weakness, formlessness, constant movement, powerfulness, and vastness. Water is used as a metaphor in the Old Testament, describing God and the desire for God in our lives.[2]

> As a deer longs for flowing streams, so my soul longs for you, O God. (Ps. 42:1)

> For my people have committed two evils: they have forsaken me, the fountain of living water. (Jer. 2:13)

> Ho, everyone who thirsts, come to the waters. (Isa. 55:1)

Those who feel isolated from God are like the ground without water:

> I stretch out my hands to you; my soul thirsts for you like a parched land. (Ps. 143:6)

Water can also be used as a symbol or metaphor for distress. In Joshua 7:5, the fearful heart melts like water. Hear the psalmist: "Save me, O God, for the waters have come up to my neck. I sink in deep mire, where there is no foothold; I have come into deep waters, and the flood sweeps over me"

(Ps. 69:1–2). And in Isaiah, God says: "Do not fear, for I have redeemed you; I have called you by name, you are mine. When you pass through the waters, I will be with you; and through the rivers , they shall not overwhelm you" (Isa. 43:1–2).

That water can be both a good and refreshing thing and a devastating thing is illustrated in this rabbinic tale: There once was a pious man who used to dig pits and cisterns to contain water for those who were traveling, those who would come and go. His daughter, on her way to her wedding, was crossing a river. She was swept away by the current. People tried to comfort the man, but he would not be comforted. The people said to the rabbi, "This is the man who has been doing such good deeds, but this cruel thing has happened to him." The rabbi said, "Is it possible that God would chastise with water a man who honored God with water?" Just then a rumor traveled through the city. "The daughter is back!" Some say that as she fell into the water, she was held up by a branch of a thorny tree. Others say that an angel in the likeness of the rabbi came down and saved her.[3]

At the beginning of the Israelites' journey, God delivers them through the waters of the Red Sea (see Ex. 14:21–22) as they leave Egypt and prepare for their journey to the land of "milk and honey." At the end of their journey, God parts the water of the Jordan River so that they can move into the land of Canaanites (see Josh. 3:7–17). The story is encased by these events of deliverance symbolized through God's control of the waters.

Water also symbolizes cleansing and healing. Various rituals in the Old Testament were performed to symbolize ritual moral purity, preparation for meeting or worshiping God. Ritual washing was required, for instance, to prepare for ordination, for the high priest's preparation for the Day of Atonement, to deal with people who had leprosy, for contact with sexual emissions, and for contact with a corpse.[4] This kind of ritual cleansing is a part of many faith traditions. For Christians, baptism marks the beginning of the ministry of Jesus and others who are called to baptism and the repentance of sin.

(Pronounce "mahn")

Manna

Wilderness. Once I asked a group of students what their first thoughts and feelings were when they heard that word. The reactions were strong and immediate and diverse. Thirst. Struggle. Loneliness. Temptation. Journey. Piercing sunlight. Those were some of the responses that were born out of life experiences fraught with decision and pain. But there were other kinds of responses as well. Revelation. Solace. Silence. One class member told about camping in the middle of the desert and seeing remarkably beautiful desert flowers that stood out from the otherwise barren and dusty existence. Another said, "The wilderness is where you are when God blesses you."

The Old Testament writers record and remember for us different sights and sounds and thoughts related to the wilderness wanderings of their Israelite ancestors. Some of those memories are very positive ones. Some not so positive. Was God there with the Israelite people? Was God not there with them? Were the people loyal to the God who had called them? Or did they, in the wilderness, abandon the God who was leading them?

The Israelites were hungry (Ex. 16:1–3). They thought life would have been easier if they had died in Egypt rather than make this grueling journey only to die away from the "comforts" of home. In response to their murmurings, Yahweh said to Moses, "I am going to rain bread from heaven for you, and each day the people shall go out and gather enough for that day" (v. 4). And Yahweh did. Described in a variety of ways, the manna that God provided to the people who did not want death was a fine, flaky substance, as fine as frost. It was not recognizable nourishment (perhaps some of the people and things God gives to us to nourish us are not immediately recognizable), melted in the hot sun, could be boiled or baked, looked like coriander seed, and was like white wafers made with honey.

Manna, or bread, is elemental to life and nourishment. It is a symbol for physical nurturing and may function as a metaphor for God's care for people as spiritual and physical beings. This food from heaven was provided by God in a situation of destitution. The people were hungry, with no provision of food in sight. They were in the desert, where a water supply was either nonexistent or severely limited. Eatable vegetation was limited, and their need for food was great. In that time and place, there were no earthly answers. An answer came from beyond them. Perhaps this is difficult for us to imagine if we have never been hungry, close to death, and in a situation that could not produce the food or water necessary for survival. In our technological age, many of us have options, and science has the answers. We get our food from stores that have received it from farmers. It can appear as if God has nothing to do with this; we address our needs without recourse to the beyond, a deity, or heavenly intervention. We are all we need.

We remember that the Israelites were in a crisis situation. They had come to the end of their resources. So destitute were they that the bondage under Pharaoh looked more appealing than freedom. Doom, despair, and hopelessness set in. And manna was provided by God for them. Manna is sign and symbol. As a sign it was visible food itself. As a symbol it pointed beyond itself to the giver. It represented God's caring presence, which we may encounter at the limits of our powers. "Manna" invites us to look not only at our resources but also at the limits of our powers. The writer of Deuteronomy says it best as he recounts for the Israelites all the ways God provided for them on their journey through the wilderness. "He humbled you by letting you hunger, then by feeding you with manna, with which neither you nor your ancestors were acquainted, in order to make you understand that one does not live by bread alone, but by every word that comes from the mouth of the LORD" (Deut. 8:3).

We learn so much about the Israelites by their response to this gift of bread. They are told to gather only enough for one day and not save it until the next; but the temptation is too great—what if there is none the next day as God has promised? They store it away, and it becomes foul and filled with worms. The Israelites are also told not to gather on the Sabbath, but some attempt to, of course. And they find none, as Yahweh has told them. Yahweh is angry. The people have gone out to gather on the day of rest. "How long will you refuse to keep my commandments and instructions?" (Ex. 16:28).

As the people traveled through the wilderness, they had a strong craving for the food that they had eaten in Egypt. They remembered the meat that they used to eat, the fish, the cucumbers, melons, leeks and onions, and the garlic. Now they had only this manna, which barely gave them enough strength to carry on. The unrealistic memories of the place where they had been slaves demonstrates how easy it is to glorify the days of the past.

For forty years, we are told, the Israelites were given this manna as they traveled through the wilderness. God was faithful in God's promise. Moses told Aaron to take a jar and put a small amount of manna in it so that it could be kept for all the generations to come. This way the children and the children's children would know how God had fed the community as it traveled. The bread was a remembrance, a token, a symbol of God's steadfastness in the face of the community's lack of faithfulness.

The loyalty and graciousness of the God who provided the manna are remembered in generations to come as the story of salvation is told and retold by the community. Ezra, in his prayer recorded in Nehemiah 9, begins by addressing the LORD who created heaven, earth, and all that is. Then he recounts all the gracious acts of God to those who committed blasphemies in the wilderness:

> You in your great mercies did not forsake them in the wilderness; the pillar of cloud that led them in the way did not leave them by day, nor the pillar of fire by night that gave them light on the way by which

they should go. You gave your good spirit to instruct them, and did not withhold your manna from their mouths, and gave them water for their thirst. Forty years you sustained them in the wilderness so that they lacked nothing; their clothes did not wear out and their feet did not swell. (Neh. 9:19–21)

Psalm 78, in a more poetic rendering of the story, says this:

Therefore, when the LORD heard, [the Lord] was full of rage; a fire was kindled against Jacob, [the Lord's] anger mounted against Israel, because they had no faith in God, and did not trust [God's] saving power. Yet [the Lord] commanded the skies above, and opened the doors of heaven; [the Lord] rained down on them manna to eat, and gave them the grain of heaven. Mortals ate of the bread of angels; [the Lord] sent them food in abundance. (Ps. 78:21–25)

It is that memory of God's willingness to continue to walk beside us and nourish us that prompts our singing of this line from "Guide Me, O Thou Great Jehovah": "Bread of heaven, feed me till I want no more."[1]

(Pronounce "mish-paht")

Justice

Justice and mercy are the attributes of God, the rabbis said. How does God exercise these divine attributes? Much as the king who had some empty goblets who said, "If I put hot water in them, they will burst. If I put cold water in, they will crack." So the king mixed cold and hot water together and poured it in, and the goblets were not harmed. Even so, God said, "If I create the world with the attribute of mercy alone, sin will multiply; if I create it with the attribute of justice alone, how can it endure? So I will create it with both, and thus it will endure."[1]

The rabbis, like us, were anxious to understand a God who could be compassionate and merciful and at the same time just. We have difficulty oftentimes holding all the attributes of God together, wondering how one does not cancel the other. The dilemma itself invites us to look more closely at this word *justice* and what it means in Old Testament narratives and prophecies.

Not surprisingly, the word *justice* grows out of a legal context. The word can mean the case before the court or the process of administering the law. It can also mean the verdict that is delivered in a certain case or the law in its abstract sense. At its root, then, the word means judging in accordance with the law. In these cases, God is the judge who executes justice and law. God is the mighty and powerful judge who is impartial and who cannot be deflected from the course of executing judgment. God executes justice for the fatherless and the widow, and God loves the stranger by giving food. God's insistence that there be justice is motivated by concern for the weak and the oppressed. God executes justice because of love for the oppressed. God judges the oppressor. God's insistence on justice is dictated by the concern for those to whom justice is denied.

I was once teaching a class on the prophetic material in the Old Testament and preaching. We were working on analyzing and interpreting the texts of the preexilic prophets. In those texts God is depicted as angry and disappointed, sometimes in grief, over the ways God's people have chosen to live in the world. On this particular day we were looking at a text in which the anger of God was provoked by the lack of justice in the world. The widows and the orphans were being ignored and not cared for. In violent and fiery language the prophet described the anger of God, which was smoking and melting the mountains (Micah 1:4; cf. Exod. 19:18). God's anger is frequently made manifest in imagery related to water or to fire. One of the students in the class asked, "Who could believe in an angry God like this one?" There was a silence in the classroom, a lengthy one. And then another student responded, "Maybe the widow and the orphan?" In that moment I knew we had learned a great lesson that would forever influence the way we looked at the anger of God. What do we think about the God who is angry at the oppression and suppression of people in this world? Perhaps that depends on whether or not we are the oppressed or the oppressor.

For this reason, the biblical command to do justice is often connected with the injunction to protect the rights of the weak and helpless. Every perversion of justice is also the imposition of suffering on someone who is unable to defend himself or herself against it.

It is, then, the recurring accusation of the prophets that the people do not champion the cause of the poor and the oppressed, that the denial of justice to the fatherless and the needy is what brings on the anger of God. It is the denial of justice that causes God to exact justice. God's anger has as its source compassion for those who, by the denial of justice, carry the burden of our sinfulness. Through the mouth of Isaiah of Jerusalem God calls out:

"Wash yourselves, make yourselves clean, Put away the evil of your doings from before mine eyes. Cease to do evil; learn to do well; seek justice, relieve the oppressed, judge the fatherless, plead for the widow" (Isa. 1:16–17, author's translation). Justice can only be done through judging the oppressor. The toleration of injustice is the toleration of human suffering. To judge, then, often becomes the equivalent of "to save"—to save the most vulnerable among us.

This explains why justice has found "comfortable company" in the Old Testament with the ideas of steadfast love, compassion, and charity. At first glance it may seem that justice would not fit in this group of words that define how we are to live in relation with our neighbor. But notice— in Jeremiah, God is called the one who "exercises loving-kindness, justice, and charity" (Jer. 9:24, author's translation).

What is this "justice," that it would be placed between love and kindness? Our Western minds have been taught to believe that justice and mercy are opposites—a judge exercises one or the other! But not so here, and not only here. The understanding of justice as being closely associated with compassion and love continually occurs. What does God require of us? Micah says to do justice and love kindness (Mic. 6:8). Hosea tells us to keep steadfast love and justice and wait for God (Hos. 12:6). Zechariah bids us to execute justice, steadfast love, and compassion to our neighbors (Zech. 8:16–17).

(Pronounce "sah-lach")

To Forgive

The Old Testament is saturated with stories of God's forgiveness. The people in the book of Judges continually fall away from Yahweh and then find their lives being lived out in the dire consequences of their actions. They cry out to Yahweh, who takes them back, and the cycle begins once again. The lamenters in the Psalms cry out for God's forgiveness, and as the psalm comes to an end, they have experienced somehow through ritual expression the forgiveness of the God who created them. Over and over the nation of Israel is forgiven by God and called back.

It is interesting that only one Hebrew word in the Old Testament is frequently translated "to forgive." Only God forgives. This verb does not describe the kind of forgiveness a person offers another, only the kind that God offers to us.

It is found only some forty-six times in the entire Old Testament. This is so, perhaps, because the Israelites used so many other expressions to describe God's relationship to us after sin. The prophets and the psalmists were creative in finding words and ways to describe what God does. God covers sin, atones for sin, removes it, lets it pass, wipes it out, washes it away, cleanses us from it, forgets it, lifts it up, and passes it by. Yahweh "throws it behind his back" (Isa. 38:17) or "throws it into the depths of the sea" (Mic. 7:19). God "heals" us from sin (Ps. 41:4).

This fullness of expression is demonstrated in Psalm 25, in which the psalmist implores Yahweh to "forgive my sin, even if it is great" (v. 11, author's translation). But with other words and in other ways this same psalmist cries out, "Be mindful of your mercy, O Lord, and of your steadfast love" (v. 6); "Do not remember the sins" (v. 7); "Turn to me and be gracious to me" (v. 16); "Consider my affliction and my trouble, and [remove] all my sins" (v. 18); and "Guard my life, and deliver me" (v. 20).[1]

Two stories depict for us the role of Moses in bringing God's forgiveness to the people. The first takes place after the people have built the golden calf in the wilderness. Moses has gone to the top of Mount Sinai and has listened to the words of Yahweh. Yahweh has given him two tablets of stone on which the finger of God had written. But while Moses is away, and because he is delayed in coming down from the top of the mount, the people have gathered around Moses' brother, Aaron, and have asked him to make gods for them. They do not know what has happened to Moses. Aaron advises them to take off their rings, and he takes the gold from them and casts an image of a calf. They worship it.

The behavior of the people does not go unnoticed by Yahweh, of course, who advises Moses to return to the people. Yahweh calls them a stiff-necked people; Yahweh is angry. Moses intercedes for the Israelite community. He asks Yahweh to "turn" from fierce wrath and change his mind. He asks Yahweh to remember the covenant Yahweh has made with Abraham and his descendants. Yahweh changes Yahweh's mind about the disaster that was being planned for the people. When the second tablet of stone is made,

Moses again intercedes and says, "O Lord, I pray, let the Lord go with us…pardon [forgive] our iniquity and our sin, and take us for your inheritance" (Ex. 34:9).

Again, in Numbers, when the people are complaining in the wilderness, Yahweh is angry that although Yahweh continues to give signs to the people, they will not believe. Yahweh threatens to strike them with pestilence and to disinherit them. But Moses, caretaker of the community, pleads for Yahweh's great name among the nations to be preserved. He says to Yahweh, "Forgive the iniquity of this people according to the greatness of your steadfast love, just as you have pardoned this people, from Egypt even until now" (Num. 14:19). And Yahweh says, "I do forgive, just as you have asked" (14:20). There are still consequences for their lack of faith, however. Those who complained and refused to obey were not allowed to enter the land that was promised them.

Leviticus offers to us an understanding of a system whereby atonement and forgiveness were made available to the community through a system of sacrifices. In chapters 4, 5, and 6, sin offerings are described. A reading of Leviticus 4:27–31 describes what should happen if an ordinary person sins unintentionally by breaking one of the commandments. When that sin is made known to the person, an offering is made of a female goat without blemish. Blood from the goat is put on the altar; the smoke of the offering will make a pleasing odor to Yahweh. Then the priest makes atonement, and "you shall be forgiven."

This refrain "you shall be forgiven" is found nine times in this and the two chapters that follow. The elaborate rituals indicate that forgiveness is possible. On the Day of Atonement all the iniquities and sins of Israel were atoned for (see Lev. 16:21, 30, 32, 34). It is this kind of forgiveness that King Solomon prayed for as the temple was dedicated in 1 Kings 8. Acknowledging the greatness of God and giving thanks for God's watchfulness, Solomon also prays for forgiveness (see 1 Kings 8:30, 34, 36, 39, 50). Reading the prayers of the Old Testament, we are invited to believe that confession has a rightful place in the worship life of the community.

(Pronounce "tz-dah-kah")

Righteousness

Righteousness may conjure images of being right, virtuous, noble, moral, ethical, upright, honest, or just. It just as often, however, conjures negative images of conceit, smugness, "holier-than-thou" attitudes; being above the fray; and rigidity. In these instances the term is used naively and defensively. Righteousness may also be associated with "righteous indignation," a form of anger that is justified because a moral boundary has been crossed or ethical norms have been violated. The opposite of righteousness is iniquitous, vicious, or corrupt.

In its Old Testament usage, righteousness is not just "being right" according to a legal, ethical, or religious norm. It is, rather, the fulfillment of the demands of relationships with another person or with God. The righteous person acts in love and maintains the covenant relationship.[1] Righteousness has a number of dimensions, including relatedness to God and accountability with others. Therefore, it is an ongoing process of understanding and growth. We do not live by our own standards; it is a reenactment of our faithfulness through our living.

The one who is righteous tries to preserve the peace and prosperity of the community by fulfilling the commands of God in regards to others. The righteous one serves God. This is the one who delivers the poor and the orphan, helps the blind along the way, supports the weak, and is the provider to the poor (Job 29:12–16). This was the righteous "clothing" in Job's life. Righteousness consists in obedience to God's law and conformity to God's nature, having mercy for the needy and helpless. Job also cared for the traveler and eschewed wealth for its own sake. The righteous one gives freely (Ps. 37:21) without regard for gain. It is not surprising that the prophets, then, called out for righteousness. It is also not surprising that the rabbis would say, "It is well with the righteous and well with his neighbor."[2]

According to the first chapters of Genesis, righteous people, those living in right relation to God and humanity, are difficult to find. Noah found favor in God's sight because Noah was a righteous man, blameless, and one who walked with God (Gen. 6:9). He lived in contrast, apparently, to all those around him; the earth was filled with corruption and with violence. And when Abraham is bargaining with God for the life of the righteous in Sodom, he pleads that the city not be destroyed if fifty righteous people are found there. God says if there are fifty righteous in the city, he will forgive the whole place. Abraham says, "If there are five less than fifty righteous people?" Then God responds, "I will not destroy them." "Thirty? Twenty? Ten?" (Gen. 18:22–33). The point is—the righteous are difficult to find. The rabbis say that "the soul of one righteous man equals in weight the entire world, all of it."[3]

> And even for the sake of just one righteous man would the world have been created. The righteous one is the foundation of the world.[4]

If righteousness is living in right relationship with God and neighbor, and if justice is seeking the welfare for the most vulnerable around us, then it is not surprising that the Old Testament prophets often speak of justice and righteousness in the same breath. They are different, yet the outcomes of both are made manifest in the same ways. They are made manifest in the way we live life with those around us.

(Pronounce "kah-vatz")

To Gather

Gathering places are important. An example in our country might be the Lincoln Memorial, site of Martin Luther King, Jr.'s, "I Have a Dream" speech and many protest marches. Westminster Abbey is a place where, for nine hundred years, people have gathered for weekly worship, weddings and funerals, and high holy days such as Christmas and Easter. It still offers hospitality to strangers, millions annually.

Gathering places, such as churches, are those places where memories are made, faith is nurtured. People come or return for orientation, a sense of direction, reaffirmation, or a sense of security. They anchor one's identity in the community. There we recollect our history and discern our collective responsibility for the present time in our quest for the unity of love, power, and justice. We gather for light; we disperse as peacemakers.

In the Old Testament people gather for many reasons: to ask Samuel for a king, to recognize David as king, and to work on the walls of Jerusalem. Troops gather and are assembled for battle. The people gather for religious functions. Jacob gathers his sons to deliver a blessing. David gathers the priests and Levites to transport the ark to Jerusalem. The people gather together to renew their covenants with God. In the prophetic books people gather together for judgment and blessing.

But perhaps most important in the Old Testament is the understanding that God is one who gathers. God pledges to assemble his people from their scattered places even before they have been scattered. This promise is repeatedly recalled by the prophets. The hope they offer to the exiles who have been taken away from their homes, native lands, customs, and religious institutions is that God is the great gatherer who will ultimately bring them back.

I will signal for them and gather them in, for I have redeemed them, and they shall be as numerous as they were before. Though I scattered them among the nations, yet in far countries they shall remember me, and they shall rear their children and return. I will bring them home from the land of Egypt, and gather them from Assyria. (Zech. 10:8–10)

See, I am going to gather them from all the lands to which I drove them in my anger and my wrath and in great indignation; I will bring them back to this place, and I will settle them in safety. They shall be my people, and I will be their God. (Jer. 32:37–38)

I will surely gather all of you, O Jacob, I will gather the survivors of Israel; I will set them together like sheep in a fold, like a flock in its pasture. (Mic. 2:12)

At that time I will bring you home, at the time when I gather you. (Zeph. 3:20)

For a brief moment I abandoned you, but with great compassion I will gather you. (Isa. 54:7)

I will gather you from the peoples, and assemble you out of the countries where you have been scattered, and I will give you the land of Israel. (Ezek. 11:17)

These few examples demonstrate how pervasive the notion of gathering is to many of the biblical prophets. There is another word in the Old Testament that means "to gather," but the word we are looking at here has a theological "ring" to it. It is used in the promises above that Israel, after being dispersed, will again be gathered into the land. And it is used in the promise that in the "great by and by" a "divine gathering" will be extended to all peoples.

I am coming to gather all nations and tongues; and they shall come and shall see my glory. (Isa. 66:18)

It is a wonderful hope and vision—that someday we will create gathering places for all people because we know we are already one people in the heart of God.

(Pronounce "koh-desh")

Holy

Holiness is a word that doesn't seem to fit well into our secular society. It brings to mind an alternative lifestyle of voluntary separation, self-denial, and religious obedience. These are values that fly in the face of a secular society that may be marked by market values, narcissistic self-absorption, and a "do your own thing" mentality. Holiness marks a voluntary break with secular assumptions and provides a lifestyle, a sacred canopy for building meaning around sacred symbols. A holiness lifestyle provides a comprehensive belief system that includes why we were born into the world, prescriptions for purposeful living, explanations for human suffering and evil, forgiveness and sanctification, comfort in dying and death, and the promise of afterlife. Few of these things can be offered by secularism.

What is the Old Testament understanding of holiness? In the sixth chapter of Isaiah, we read about the call of the prophet. He is standing in the temple in the year that King Uzziah died. He sees Yahweh sitting on a throne, high and lofty. Seraphs attend Yahweh, each one having six wings. One calls out to the other and says, "Holy, holy, holy is the LORD of hosts; the whole earth is full of his glory" (Isa. 6:3). The vision is filled with the temple's shaking foundations and with smoke, each adding to the mystery. The prophet calls out, "Woe is me, I am lost, for I am a man of unclean lips, and I live among a people of unclean lips; yet my eyes have seen the King, the LORD of hosts!" (Isa. 6:5)

In this story we come to a clear understanding of the meaning of *holy* in the Old Testament. Holy means separate from that which is common. Holy means awesome. It means to have a character that is totally good, without evil or sin. It means in some sense to be "connected" with the Divine. It is no wonder, then, that the prophet, sensing this One who is holy, comes suddenly to realize and verbalize his own inadequacies and uncleanness. "Woe is me!" In fact, Isaiah of Jerusalem comes to realize not only his own sinfulness but that of the entire community that surrounds him. This he comes to recognize when he sees God. We sing about this kind of God, "Holy, holy, holy. Lord God Almighty! Early in the morning our song shall rise to thee…cherubim and seraphim falling down before thee…perfect in power, in love, and purity."[1]

In Isaiah and in the Psalms, God is frequently referred to as holy or as the Holy One of Israel. Places where God is worshiped are referred to as holy places. When Moses stands at the burning bush (Ex. 3), he hears Yahweh calling his name, "Moses, Moses." He is told to take off his shoes, for the place on which he is standing is "holy ground." When Jacob receives his vision in the city of Bethel, he consecrates it as a holy place (Gen. 28:11–22). The temple in Jerusalem came to be one of the most holy places in Israel because it was the dwelling place for God (1 Kings 8:10–11). The altars, candleholders, vestments, musical instruments, and so forth within the temple were considered holy because they were separated, or set aside, for holy use. (The word *holy* is used more than a hundred times in Exodus and Leviticus, where the description of the liturgical elements for the temple are described.) The distinction between things that were in the sphere of sacred, and thus holy, and those things that were common and of the world had to be maintained. "Remember the sabbath day to keep it holy." That means the sabbath day was different, separate, of a different realm. It was not to be treated like other common days. The priests were holy; their words and rituals were holy.

The inner sanctum of the temple was known as the "Holy of Holies." It was a protected place, dark, that housed the ark of the covenant. It represented God's divine presence and the relationship God had with Israel. Although the Israelites did not believe that God's presence could be confined to any particular place or building, the Ark served as a visible reminder that God was near. Israel was a holy nation. The Holiness Code, the list of ritual and ethical laws, was the means by which the people would maintain their holiness.

It is a complicated notion—holiness. Theologians have tried to understand the difference between being in the world and not of the world. They have tried to understand the difference between sacred space and other space. There does seem to be merit in coming to some understanding of what it means to be "of God" in a world that often is not. Our answers to what might be holy behavior, motives, attitudes, and lifestyles might differ from our ancestors of faith; they might even be subversive. But to be holy—of the sacred—requires intentionality and a life of prayer and of study. That is what we sing about in the well-known hymn "Take Time to Be Holy":

> Take time to be holy; speak oft with thy Lord;
> abide in him always, and feed on his word.
> Make friends of God's children; help those who
>   are weak;
> forgetting in nothing God's blessing to seek.[2]

Even in the first verse of the hymn there are different thoughts and ideas about how one might go about living the holy/sacred life: prayer, studying the Word, being friends with God's children, helping those who are vulnerable, seeking God's presence and blessing.

(Pronounce "kah-vah")

To Wait

It is surprising, really, but there is no Hebrew word in the Old Testament that is consistently translated "hope." There are several words sometimes translated "hope," but more often they are translated "to wait." In some ways this is a puzzle to us, because we may see hoping as a very positive thing, that which sustains us, whereas waiting is something less than ideal. Who wants to wait? It is like being put on hold. It is associated with being passed over by more important priorities. We feel good when we do not have to wait, frustrated when we do. "Why wait?" we might ask ourselves. Waiting makes us anxious, frustrated, or angry. We may give up because we want things to happen on time, our time. We want the world to be orderly and predictable. We want to be first, and we want instant results.

These associations with the word *wait* are demonstrated clearly by Martin Luther King, Jr., when he spoke during the civil rights movement about how "to wait" often meant "never." "For years now we have heard the word 'wait!' It rings in the ear of every Negro with piercing familiarity. This 'wait' has almost always meant 'never.' We must come to see, with one of our most distinguished jurists, that 'justice too long delayed is justice denied.'"[1]

In another sense, however, the association between hoping and waiting makes all the sense in the world. One waits only when there is hope. If there is no hope, one no longer waits.

Waiting has some positive associations also. Waiting can be part of a disciplined action. It may offer insight and opportunities that one would otherwise miss if life were in constant motion. Waiting offers us opportunities to rest, to contemplate, or to revisit a decision. It may allow time for someone else to "catch up." It may teach us patience and allow us to still ourselves and be in the presence of God. The prayers and the eschatological visions of a better day to come speak to this kind of waiting.

Isaiah 25 begins with shouts of thanksgiving to a God who throughout history has been with God's people. This is a God who is old, faithful, and sure. This is one who can be trusted. Yahweh is like a refuge to the poor and needy, the shelter from the rainstorm, the shade from the heat—each of these metaphors gives the reader a sense of the comfort that Yahweh can provide.

Verses 6–10a give a description of the wonderful day to come. The brief images provide an assortment of rich and poignant pictures of what that day will be. The vision takes place on a mountain. Yahweh will make there a banquet for *all* peoples. It is a feast rich with foods and wines. This will be the place where the death that has swallowed women and men will now itself be swallowed. Tears will be wiped away; disgrace will be taken away from all the earth. The people will be aware of the presence of Yahweh, who has provided the bounty and the relief for them. It is in the refrain (v. 9) that we become aware that this wonderful confirmation of God's presence and care is not unanticipated. The people have *waited* for God to save them. Again in verse 9 it is emphasized that the One who has come is the One for whom the people have waited. They will be glad and rejoice.

This idea of waiting for Yahweh is common in the book of Psalms. The prayers there often sing about waiting for God.

Do not let those who wait for you be put to shame. (Ps. 25:3)

But those who wait for the LORD shall inherit the land. (37:9)

For you I wait all day long. (25:5)

> May integrity and uprightness preserve me, for I wait
> for you. (25:21)

It is with expectation that the people of Yahweh have waited
for this day when salvation will come to all peoples.

The people wait for Yahweh, and they will not be
disappointed. The story in Isaiah 25 ends with a note of
confident assurance and, therefore, one of comfort. This joyful
confirmation of the people's hope and expectation brings to
the reader of Isaiah an ironic twist, a sad reality that cannot
be shaken. In the song of the vineyard (Isaiah 5), Yahweh
also waits expectantly. Yahweh waits for the field to yield
good grapes (5:2). Yahweh waits hopefully and expectantly
for justice, but looking on the world Yahweh sees only
bloodshed. Yahweh waits for the righteousness, but hears
only the cries of the oppressed (v. 7). Yahweh waits. Yahweh
is disappointed. The people who wait for Yahweh, however,
are never disappointed. Their confidence has not been
misplaced.

(Pronounce "roo-ach")

Spirit

Wind. Breath. Spirit. The word *ruach* can be translated in
any of these ways. It can mean literally the wind that sweeps
across Palestine from the east or from the west—a cool
refreshing wind—or the hot dry winds that can, in only a
matter of minutes, turn the earth into a parched wasteland.
It can describe that which, like the wind, either moves or
causes something to move. It can also mean, however, the

living quality of life itself that was once breathed into women and men at their creation.

We are introduced to this word in the first verses of the first chapter of the first book of the Old Testament. "In the beginning when God created the heavens and the earth, the earth was a formless void and darkness covered the face of the deep, while a wind from God [or while the spirit of God] swept over the face of waters" (Gen. 1:1–2). God's spirit moves and creation begins; it was there from the beginning. This spirit is a birthing, creative one; in Hebrew it is feminine in gender. She moves, and creation begins; she is active and can bring dead bones to life, intercede when words fail us, guide us into paths of faithful service, and transform us. This wind, breath, force, power, and vitality, whether human or divine, empowers and overpowers. She authorizes us for ministry; she looses and liberates us from the forces that might bind us.[1]

This wind or spirit or breath of God moves about in the world in a mysterious fashion. Like wind and breath, it cannot be seen; only its consequences are discernible to the human eye. But it is not a purposeless movement that we witness in the spirit's moving. It has function, and it has purpose; it is wind in motion.

In the Old Testament a person's spirit can be sad, overwhelmed, contrite, cool, restrained, jealous, patient, or proud. People may have a spirit of wisdom or of whoredom. The work of God's spirit may be cosmic, creative, providential, redemptive, indwelling, or infilling; it can provide for leadership or service and can empower.[2]

We see three major emphases of the spirit in the Old Testament. The first is the spirit as an agent of creation. The second is the spirit as a source of power and inspiration for the judges, kings, and prophets. The latter, because they possess or are possessed by this spirit, speak and act to bring a word from Yahweh. The third emphasis is on God's presence in the community.

It is interesting to watch the spirit at work in all these various ways. In the book of Judges the spirit of Yahweh comes upon the judges who are called forth to deliver and lead the Israelites out of their troubles and back into relationship with God. The stories are fascinating, as one by one seemingly ordinary persons are called forth to do extraordinary things. Find these verses (Judg. 3:10; 6:34; 11:29; 13:25; 14:6, 19; 15:14) and read the stories of Othniel, Gideon, and the rest. Revel in their heroics and the humor and tragedy of their stories. It was the spirit of Yahweh that brought them forward into service.

So, too, the writing prophets were visited by the spirit of God. Ezekiel describes the experience this way: "He said to me: O mortal, stand up on your feet, and I will speak with you. And when he spoke to me, a spirit entered into me and set me on my feet; and I heard him speaking to me" (Ezek. 2:1–2). Throughout the early chapters of Ezekiel the spirit enters Ezekiel, takes him up, lifts him, falls, is poured upon him, and carries him as he goes about his proclaiming and prophesying to the Israelites in exile.

The spirit can also come upon the community. The word of hope from the prophets reads:

> Therefore say: Thus says the Lord GOD: I will gather you from the peoples, and assemble you out of the countries where you have been scattered, and I will give you the land of Israel. When they come there, they will remove from it all its detestable things and all its abominations. I will give them one heart, and put a new spirit within them; and I will remove the heart of stone from their flesh and give them a heart of flesh. (Ezek. 11:17–19)

The spirit is a gift from God given to those who were scattered and are now gathered home.

> The spirit of the Lord GOD is upon me, because the LORD has anointed me; [the Lord] has sent me to bring good news to the oppressed, to bind up the brokenhearted, to proclaim liberty to the captives, and release to the prisoners; to proclaim the year of the LORD's favor, and the day of vengeance of our God; to comfort all who mourn. (Isa. 61:1–2)

It is the spirit of God who empowers us to be about God's liberating work in the world, as the psalms express:

Create in me a clean heart, O God, and put a new and right spirit within me. Do not cast me away from your presence, and do not take your holy spirit from me. Restore to me the joy of your salvation, and sustain in me a willing spirit. (Ps. 51:10–12)

The spirit represents the longing that we have to live our life in good and productive and life-giving ways.

Howard Thurman writes about this in *The Centering Moment.*

It is good to remember that God has not left [God's self] without a witness in our spirits, that despite all of the wanderings of our footsteps, despite all of the ways by which we have sought to circumvent [God's] truth in us, despite all of the weaknesses of spirit and of mind and of resoluteness and of body, despite all of the blunders by which we have isolated ourselves from our fellows and proven unworthy of the love and the trust and the confidence by which again and again our faltering lives are surrounded, despite all of this, it is good to remember that God has not left [God's self] without a witness in our lives.[3]

(Pronounce "rah-cham")

To Have Compassion

The story in 1 Kings 3:16–28 demonstrates clearly the wisdom of King Solomon. Two prostitutes come and stand before him. One of them says to him, "Please, my lord, this woman and I live in the same house; and I gave birth while she was in the house. Then on the third day after I gave birth, this woman also gave birth. We were together; there was no one else with us in the house, only the two of us were in the house. This woman's son died in the night because she lay on him. She got up in the middle of the night and took my son from beside me while your servant slept. She laid him at her breast and laid her dead son at my breast. When I rose in the morning to nurse my son, I saw that he was dead; but when I looked at him closely in the morning, clearly it was not the son I had borne." An argument follows. Each of the two women claims the living son as her own.

The dilemma is clearly set before the king; the difficulty of making a sound and fair judgment is evident. The king orders a sword and says, "Divide the living boy in two; then give half to the one, and half to the other." The true mother cries out, wanting to save the life of her child; through the love for her child she has been exposed. The storyteller explains her actions this way: "because compassion for her son burned within her" (v. 26).

It is the word *compassion* that interests us here. In its singular form the Hebrew word *rechem* means "womb" or "uterus." In the plural, it means compassion, mercy, and love. The womb protects and nourishes, but it does not possess and control. It yields so that wholeness and well-being may happen. Through this story we not only understand the wisdom of the king but also the compassion of a loving mother.

It is not only women, of course, who know this kind of compassion. Joseph feels this compassion burning inside himself when he first meets his brother Benjamin, son of his mother (Gen. 43:30, 45:14). Ultimately we come to understand that the love of the prostitute for her child and the love Joseph has for his brother is the same kind of compassion that God has for us. Isaiah (49:15) uses this word to speak of a mother's love toward her nursing child and, consequently, God's love for us. The psalms use it to describe the love of a father and, ultimately, God's love for us. "As a father has compassion for his children, so [Yahweh] has compassion for those who fear [Yahweh]" (Ps. 103:13). The word names the kind of feeling that people have for one another simply by virtue of the fact that they are human beings. This kind of compassion is most easily prompted by infants or anyone who is helpless.

God shows compassion, this strong tie, with those called God's children. While the message of the Old Testament prophets is one of judgment and one that calls the people back to relationship with God, it just as surely proclaims a message of forgiveness and compassion from Yahweh.

> And after I have plucked them up, I will again have compassion on them, and I will bring them again to their heritage and to their land, every one of them. (Jer. 12:15)

> But the LORD will have compassion on Jacob and will again choose Israel, and will set them in their own land. (Isa. 14:1)

> Who is a God like you, pardoning iniquity and passing over the transgression of the remnant of your possession? [God] does not retain [God's] anger forever, because [God] delights in showing clemency. God will again have compassion upon us; [God] will tread our iniquities under foot. You will cast all our sins into the depths of the sea. (Mic. 7:18–19)

Two stories from the rabbis help us to evaluate our own sense and understanding of compassion and the way we are to live out the deep, tender, merciful compassion of Yahweh toward the people, a womb-like kind of love that a mother has for a child.

> Once a pious rabbi failed to appear in the synagogue for worship on the holy Eve of Atonement. The members of his congregation went out to search for him and found him in the barn of a neighbor. What happened to keep him from leading the congregation in prayer? On the way to the synagogue he found a neighbor's calf lost and tangled in the brush. Fearing that he might hurt the animal, he freed it tenderly

and brought it back to its stall. He was asked, "How could you do that? Your first duty as a rabbi is prayer." The rabbi answered, "God is called *rachamono*, the Merciful One. An act of compassion is a prayer, too."[1]

A former chief rabbi of Jerusalem, a sage, accorded loving-kindness to heretics, freethinkers, thieves, charlatans, and hypocrites, basing himself on the assumption that man is but little lower than angels, and that there is a spark of saintliness in every human being. A disciple protested: "They don't deserve your time. They are taking advantage of your goodness." "My son," replied the rabbi, "it is much better to be guilty of groundless love than groundless hate. We are commanded to imitate the attributes of God. If God has compassion upon all God's creatures, should I close my ear and withhold my pity from any God has created?"[2]

(Pronounce "rah-phah")

To Heal

We look for healing after we recognize that something is broken, injured, or not right. Healing is the process of restoring to health or soundness, to set right or to repair, to come to wholeness. Our healings can be emotional, physical, psychological, spiritual, and relational. "Healing" implies a process of overcoming, a yet and a not yet. "Healed" is past tense; the process has been completed, and our scars are the evidence that injury has been overcome. They are the marker that healing has taken place.

The Hebrews had an understanding of the world as good. There was a unity of mind and body created by God; health was viewed as a blessing. Oftentimes it was seen as a reward for righteousness and faithfulness to God. Illness was sometimes seen as a punishment for wrongdoings. There was, then, this understanding of the relatedness of holiness, a centered and covenanted life, righteousness, healing, salvation, and peace.[1]

The church has shown a continued interest in healing throughout the centuries. Prayers, confession, the sacraments, meditation, and many Christian practices are used to facilitate healing. The tradition has acknowledged a spiritual dimension to healing and that bodily wholeness, emotional well-being, mental functioning, and spiritual health are related in important ways.

We look for healing in many ways and in all sorts of places, but those in despair, singing their songs of lament recorded in our book of Psalms, found healing in God.

Their cries for healing are piercing. "O LORD, do not rebuke me in your anger, or discipline me in your wrath. Be gracious to me, O LORD, for I am languishing; O LORD, heal me, for my bones are shaking with terror" (Ps. 6:1–2). The one who speaks is worried that death is imminent. He is weary from moaning, and every night he floods his bed with tears; his eyes waste away because of grief. He is overwhelmed by the work of his enemies, and he is afraid.

Psalm 41 begins with an affirmation that Yahweh considers the poor, delivers them and keeps them alive, sustains them on their sickbed, and heals them. The psalmist then calls out for the same. "O LORD, be gracious to me; heal me, for I have sinned against you" (Ps. 41:4). This seems at first to be a confession, and perhaps it is. But the psalmist also needs to be healed, because the enemy whispers things about him. Even his friend, the one in whom he trusted and who ate with him, has betrayed him.

Psalm 60 is a prayer for restoration. The community has been rejected, perhaps devastated in war. God is angry with them. "You have caused the land to quake; you have torn it open; [heal the breaches] in it, for it is tottering" (Ps. 60:2). It is the war-torn, perhaps earthquake-ridden community in need of healing. These examples show that it is not only the individual's physical condition that needs to be healed. It is the relationship she has with and the way she stands before God. Healing can be tied to forgiveness and to restoration and to deliverance.

Just as there are piercing cries for healing, there are also joyous affirmations that healing does take place. "How good it is to sing praises to our God; for [God] is gracious, and a song of praise is fitting. The LORD builds up Jerusalem... gathers the outcasts of Israel...heals the brokenhearted and binds up their wounds" (Ps. 147:1–3). The laments in the Old Testament often end with a rousing chorus of assurance that God has heard the plea of the one in distress and that God will bring deliverance, salvation, or healing. There is for this psalmist that rousing assurance that God heals those who have broken hearts.

There is another word for healing in the Old Testament, but it is used far less frequently than this one, and it comes from a root meaning "long" or "lengthen," which signifies the life that is prolonged or lengthened. The verbal form is used in Deuteronomy frequently where the people are given ordinances or commandments that they are to follow so that "it may be well with you and that you may 'prolong' your days in the land"(see Deut. 5:16, 11:21, and 25:15). There were ways to go about living and ways to be in relationship with God that would give one a long life.

This second word for healing is used in Jeremiah, first to describe the despair of the prophet that the community has not experienced healing by Yahweh (Jer. 8:22), and later in words from Yahweh to the community, promising restoration: "For I will restore health to you, and your wounds I will heal, says the LORD" (30:17). Yahweh speaks of the recovery that will come to the city that has been devastated by war: "I am going to bring it recovery and healing; I will heal them and reveal to them abundance of prosperity and security" (33:6).

It is the use of this word for healing in Isaiah 58 that is perhaps the most striking. Yahweh, through the prophet, is describing how an acceptable life to Yahweh is to be lived. Beginning in verse 6 there is a powerful statement about the expectations God has for the people who are living in community with one another. Fasting for fasting's sake is not acceptable. Yahweh prefers that the people loosen the bonds of injustice and work for freedom for those who are oppressed. Yahweh prefers not fasting, but shared bread, the homeless housed, the naked clothed. When these are done, "Then your light shall break forth like the dawn, and your healing shall spring up quickly" (Isa. 58:8). This is a portrait of a communal healing. This is a healing that comes not to individuals but to a group of people who are working together for one another's health and well-being. It is a portrait of a community being responsible for and making a priority of the most vulnerable among them. In such a place, healing springs up—quickly.

When you do these things, the prophet continues, the light rises. Yahweh will guide you and satisfy your needs in parched places and make your bones strong. Water will quench your thirst. Ruins will be rebuilt, and many generations will follow. "You shall be called the repairer of the breach, the restorer of streets to live in" (58:12). The people who work toward restoration of all humanity are given this new name. It is a fulfillment of their calling.

It is to this kind of ministry that the contemporary church is called—to be a healing presence in the modern world wherever healing is needed. That might be between cultures, races, generations, genders, orientations, religious traditions, or within oneself and one's family. As in the texts of old, healing is associated with salvation, peace, holiness, righteousness, and justice. The church is called to be about the business of healing not only persons but also society, the world, the system that creates inequities and prejudices under which people suffer. This is the bringing together of the social, political, economic, and ecological dimensions of health and healing with the spiritual, emotional, and physical. Thus, Isaiah 58 rings out an ancient and a contemporary plea:

Remove the yokes, offer your food, meet the needs of the afflicted.

In looking about the world and its need for good health and healing, we might despair at the needs and be inclined to call out as Jeremiah did: "Is there no balm in Gilead? Is there no physician there? Why then has the health [healing] of my poor people not been restored?" (Jer. 8:22). Perhaps we are called out into the world to do that healing work.

(Pronounce "shah-vath")

To Cease or Rest

This verb means basically to sever, cease, put an end to, or rest. This verb is used about seventy times in the Old Testament to describe, for instance, the fact that day and night shall never cease or that the seed of Israel shall not cease from being a nation. It describes the three friends of Job who finally ceased to answer their friend. The verb is used of God, who causes the arrogancy of the proud to cease or will cause wars to cease until the end of the earth. When the middle consonant of the word is doubled (this is indicated by a dot in the middle letter—*shabbath*), the word becomes "Sabbath." What is the significance of this day, and for what reasons was it called into being by the Israelites? Why is it important?

The end of the first creation story in Genesis 1 supplies the reason for the observance of Sabbath. God ceases from the work of creation that has taken six days. The seventh day is then blessed and called holy. This day of rest became the cornerstone of Israelite religious practice. It is mentioned repeatedly throughout the Pentateuch (the first five books of the Old Testament), and occasionally the kinds of work that are prohibited on that day are recounted: gathering food, plowing, reaping, kindling a fire, and chopping wood.

Perhaps because of a need to preserve the nation's unique identity among other nations, the idea of Sabbath became very important during the days of the prophets. Jeremiah attaches the fate of Jerusalem to its observance (Jer. 17:27). Third Isaiah singles out the keeping of the Sabbath as that which will bring personal and national salvation (Isa. 56:1–6)).[1]

The calls to celebrate and honor the Sabbath are found in Exodus 23:12; 31:15; and 20:10. In the first instances the reasons for celebrating the Sabbath are stated positively: "Six days you shall work but on the seventh you shall rest." In the latter, "You shall not work on the Sabbath." Throughout the Old Testament several reasons are given for this day of rest. First (Ex. 20:11) we are told that the observance is related to God's resting on the seventh day after six days of creative work. It is almost as if the first creation story is told so that the institution of Sabbath-keeping could be maintained. It is an invitation to rejoice in the goodness of the created world and to recognize God's sovereignty over it.

In Deuteronomy 5:15, Sabbath-keeping is related to the great story of deliverance from Egypt: "You shall remember that you were a slave in the land of Egypt, and Yahweh your God brought you out with a mighty hand… therefore, Yahweh your God commanded you to keep the sabbath day" (author's translation). Thus, every Sabbath, Israel is to remember that God is the one who redeems and delivers.

The third reason given for Sabbath-keeping, however, is a social, humanitarian, justice-seeking reason. The Sabbath is to be a day that affords dependent laborers a day of rest, so that "your ox and your ass" may have rest and the "son of your bondsmaid and the alien" may be refreshed (see Ex. 20:10; 23:12; Deut 5:14–15). Here, the commandment to keep the Sabbath seems to be an effort to make all equal under God. As the Sabbath recalls the liberation from Egypt, so it in turn must become an agent of freedom, of liberation, by setting people free, if only for a few hours.

Last, keeping the Sabbath honors a sign of the covenant. The Sabbath joins with the signs of the rainbow and circumcision (see Ex. 31:13; Num. 15:32–36; Jer. 17:19–27). Keeping the Sabbath means keeping one's loyalty to Yahweh.[2]

Many stories developed in Jewish tradition about the keeping of the Sabbath and the importance of doing so. A story is told of a pious man who took a walk in his vineyard on the Sabbath. When he noticed a breach in the fence, he resolved to repair it when the Sabbath was over. But then he said, "Since the thought of repairing it came to me on the Sabbath, I will need to leave it unrepaired. Forever." How did the Holy One reward him? A big caper bush grew up in the vineyard and filled the breach in the fence, and with the fruit of that bush he sustained himself for the rest of his life.[3] Through this story the importance of keeping the Sabbath was reinforced. Although the understandings of why the Sabbath should be kept varied according to scripture, writing and thinking about its importance were important tasks for the rabbis.

How does one learn about the Sabbath? God provides many ways, as this humorous story recounts: There once was a man who had a heifer. In time, the pious man lost his wealth, and he had to sell his heifer to a heathen, who plowed with her for six days of the week. But on the Sabbath, when he brought her out, she lay down under the yoke and would not work. Though he kept beating her, she would not budge from her place. He went to the pious man and said to him, "Take back your heifer. For six days I worked her. When I took her out on the Sabbath, she lay down under the yoke and would not work. And though I beat her again and again, she would not budge from her place."

When the heathen said this, the pious man understood that the reason she would do no work was because she had become accustomed to rest on the Sabbath. He said, "Come along, I will get her up and make her plow." When he came to her, he whispered in her ear, "Heifer, when you were in my possession, you rested on the Sabbath. But now that my sins have forced me to sell you to this heathen, I beg you to stand up and do the will of your new master." At once she stood up and was ready to do the work. The heathen said to the pious man, "I won't let you go until you tell me what you did to her and what you whispered into her ear. Did you perhaps practice some sorcery upon her?" The pious man told the heathen what he had said.

The heathen was both amazed and shaken, and he said, "If this creature that has no speech, no intelligence affirms her Creator, shall not I, whom the Holy One created in His own image and likeness, and into whom He put cognition and intelligence—shall I not affirm the Creator?" At once he became a proselyte. He was privileged to study Torah and came to be called "son of a heifer."[4]

There was in the Jewish community, as there became in the Christian community, an effort to determine what could and could not be done on the Sabbath. Could, for instance, wine and oil be "beaten" for a sick person so that the person could be made well? One rabbi thought so, but went on to tell about the time another rabbi had a pain in his stomach, and as the others were about to mix oil and wine for him, he would not permit it.[5]

(Pronounce "shoov")

To Return

"To return" means many things. Return marks our beginning and our end, our start and finish. From the dust of the earth we were formed, and to the dust we shall return. The idea of return indicates that we are a pilgrim people, a people on the move, a people who journey from one place to another. We return to search for something we have lost. To return is to revisit a place of former involvement. Hence, "the place" to which we return takes on importance. That place may be geographical or a memory or an idea or a relationship. To return is to remember former things, but from a standpoint that is different from the original one.

It might be surprising to find out that "to return" is the twelfth most frequently used verb in the Old Testament! It is used in many of the ways we would use the word: to describe a person who goes on a journey and then returns home, to describe a person who borrows an object and then returns it. It can mean to carry or bring back. But the theological context of the word *shuv* is most interesting. It means something like repentance, the turning back to God.

The Bible talks about repentance and uses a variety of images and metaphors to describe and call it forth. People are asked to incline their hearts to Yahweh (Josh. 24:23; 1 Kings 8:58), circumcise themselves to God (Deut. 10:16; 30:6; Jer. 4:4), wash their hearts from wickedness (Jer. 4:14), and so forth. But the one expression that overshadows all these others is the call to return.

When in the contemporary world we use the word *repentance,* different scenarios come to mind. Often repentance is associated with emotional outbursts—evangelists standing before television audiences of millions, confessing sins, and pleading for mercy. This is not unlike the portrait painted by the psalmist in Psalm 51, who calls on the steadfast love of God to blot out transgressions, wash iniquity, and cleanse sin. The psalmist asks for a clean heart and a new and right spirit; the psalmist wants to be assured of God's continuing presence with him. The psalmist wants to teach others what he has learned; he wants others to return to God (Ps. 51:13).

But when the word *return* is used to describe repentance, it means something more. It is this word that is most often used by the Old Testament prophets to call people back. They do not call for simply an emotional outpouring and a confession of sin and iniquity, but for something more active and more intentional, a refocusing and a movement in a different direction, away from something (evil) and toward something (God).

Although the prophets issue the strong and compelling calls to return to God, the language of the emotional appeals varies. With different language come different understandings and perceptions and thoughts about God. We find this verb more often in Jeremiah (111 times) than in any other Old Testament book. Jeremiah 3, for instance, has an appeal for faithless Israel to return (v. 12). Yahweh says that Yahweh will not look on Israel in anger, but with mercy. Yahweh indicates that the anger will not last forever; the community needs to acknowledge its guilt and rebellion. Again in verse 14 the plea to return comes to the faithless children, a plea that is repeated in verse 22: "Return, O faithless children, I will heal your faithlessness." The repetition of the imperative call to return comes from a God anxious for the people to be restored and to begin relationship anew and aright.

The pleas from Amos in chapter 4 have an angry flavor. The God portrayed here is an exasperated God who seems to have tried everything to get the attention of God's people. Yahweh has withheld bread from them, "yet you did not return to me" (Amos 4:6). Yahweh withheld rain from them, "yet you did not return to me" (vv. 7–8). The people were struck with blight and mildew, "yet you did not return to me" (v. 9). They lost in battle, "yet you did not return to me." (v. 10). They were overthrown, and God repeats, "yet you did not return to me" (v. 11). This recounting of the drastic things Yahweh has done ends with this declaration: "Prepare to meet your God" (v. 12). If the people will not come to God, God will come to them.

While these appeals from the prophets may leave us with varied feelings about the God who calls us forth, we see a longing for the renewal of a relationship that God and the community once enjoyed. To return to God is to know that when we have walked away, God is there when we decide to come home. And when we return, we become the living testament or memorial to the steadfast love of a God who is waiting for us. It is not, "Turn around and come home and then I will love you." It is, "I love you. Turn around; come home."

There is a hopefulness in the notion of returning. Inherent in it is the understanding that it is possible to change, to redirect, and to make a movement in a different direction. And so the prophets among us have called and continue to call us out, call us back, call us home, call us to return to the God who created and loves us. Sometimes we do not even know we have left; it is easy to seduce ourselves into thinking that our way of living is God's way. "Have we left?" we might ask ourselves. "When did we wander away?"

(Pronounce "shah-lohm")

Peace

Prosperity. Health. Peace. Wellness. Completeness. Safety. Harmony. Satisfaction. Fulfillment. Unity. Victory. Restoration. There is not just one word that translates adequately the Hebrew word *shalom*. It means more than the absence of war, more than inner calm. *Shalom,* the sense that one has "enough," can be both internal and external; it can come because of one's material resources or because of one's inner strength. In the Old Testament, shalom comes when the payment is made to a conqueror or when a business transaction is complete. It can come when payment of a vow is made and both parties are in a state of shalom. When an obligation is met, a kind of wholeness is restored. With the debt cancelled, life goes on. Mostly, however, shalom is a state of being that comes from the result of God's presence.

God as the source of *shalom* is of most interest to us here. Many of us have often cited and recited the blessing that Yahweh gave to Moses and that Moses was to give to Aaron and his sons. Aaron was to bless the Israelites with these words: "The LORD bless you and keep you; the LORD make his face to shine upon you, and be gracious to you; the LORD lift up his countenance upon you, and give you peace" (Num. 6:24–26) In the giving of peace, Yahweh does these things: blesses, guards or keeps, treats graciously, and lifts Yahweh's countenance upon the gathered community. What does it mean for Yahweh to lift Yahweh's countenance upon us?

In the prophetic books of the Old Testament there is a cry from Yahweh to the world that we learn to recognize when there is peace and when there is not. It would seem that peace would be self-evident. In Micah 3, for instance, the indictment of the people is that they do not "know justice." They hate good and love evil. The imagery used to describe the way the community goes about its living is quite graphic. They "tear the skin off" the people, pull the flesh from bone. They flay and break and chop those around them. Ultimately, the indictment is on the prophets who have brought an easy word to the community and who have led the people astray. They have taught the fortunate ones to cry "peace" when they have something to eat, even though there are others who have nothing (Mic. 3:1–5). In Jeremiah and in Ezekiel, accusation is brought against those who would cry out "Peace, peace" when there is none (Jer. 6:14; 8:11; Ezek. 13:10). The people are easily seduced into thinking the world is "right" when their own little corner of it is "right." These kinds of prophets "whitewash" the truth so that their words will be easy to hear. When peace is proclaimed and there is still unrest, wounds cannot be healed. Jeremiah says that this kind of word "treats the wounds carelessly."

Peace is not always something that mysteriously settles into one's soul. In the Old Testament, peace is something that is sought, pursued, made, and spoken. It takes energy and persistence and a great amount of effort to beat swords into plowshares. Peace is intimately associated with truth-telling (Esth. 9:30; Isa. 39:8; Jer. 33:6; Zech. 8:16, 19) and is related to righteousness—our willingness to go about living in godly ways.

Psalm 85 presents to us a grand and glorious vision of the way the world can and will be. At the conclusion of a rousing call for help from God, the psalmist paints a picture of the response from God when the call is an urgent plea to see God's steadfast love and to be granted salvation (Ps. 85:7):

> Let me hear what God the LORD will speak, for he will speak peace to his people, to his faithful, to those who turn to him in their hearts. Surely his salvation is at hand for those who fear him, that his glory may dwell in our land. Steadfast love and faithfulness will meet; righteousness and peace will kiss each other. (vv. 8–10)

Righteousness and peace will kiss. *Shalom* is created on the earth when we are righteous; it has something to do with the way we choose to live life with one another. Peace is more than just the absence of war and strife. This peace is driven by love and justice, with its benefit of an undisturbed, productive, and anxiety-free life for all.[1]

This must be what Dr. Martin Luther King, Jr., meant when he wrote about peace.

> True peace is not merely the absence of tension, but it is the presence of justice. Peace is one of the most talked about, perhaps least understood and sought after states of our time or of any time, and yet it is almost impossible to achieve or to maintain. What is peace? Is it a dream state from which we must awake? No. It may not be something we ever really achieve, but something we continuously strive for. For as long as there is inequality and people are starving, naked and homeless, do not have the basic necessities and lack dignity, then there is not peace. It requires the presence of justice, love and power.[2]

(Pronounce "shah-mah")

To Hear

The exodus story begins with a human cry that rises up to God. God hears the Israelites who groan under their oppressors, and the great story of deliverance begins to unfold. Moses is keeping watch over sheep. He glimpses the flames of the burning bush. Turning aside to see this strange message, Moses hears a voice calling to him by name and responds, "Here I am." Yahweh speaks to him, comforting, or perhaps warning, that he is standing on holy ground. He is called to bring Yahweh's people out of Egypt. Twice Moses is reminded that Yahweh has heard the people's cry. The speaker is a *listening* God (Ex. 3).

We travel with the Israelites on their journey through the desert. And now Moses stands in the wilderness on the east side of the Jordan River. He and the Israelites have, at long last, completed their grueling and circuitous journey. They stand looking at the land they have sought for decades. Moses, knowing that he will not be allowed to make that final step into the land of the Canaanites, stands to speak to the community just as Yahweh instructed. One can imagine the exhilaration and sadness with which Moses brought forth his farewell address. There must have been so much he wanted to say to his people; there would be so much he would want them to remember. He would want them to recall how God had been with them on the journey. He would want them to remember how they were to go about being God's people in a new and foreign land. He would want them to renew the covenant they had made with God. He would want them to be faithful. Cast as his last words to the thronging crowds standing before him, Deuteronomy brings us the words of farewell.

Before the recounting of the laws, Moses reminds the people of the experience they had on Mount Horeb when they approached the mountain and Yahweh spoke to them. Remember, he tells them, there was only a voice. In the story the laws are given not through writing, but through speech. The laws were written on tablets of stone after the people had first heard them. The voice of God was so frightening that the people thought that to hear it would mean death. Here, the spoken word defined and formed the covenant.

Even the casual reader of the book of Deuteronomy will realize that "hearing" is of fundamental importance to the Israelite faith. The Shema in Deuteronomy 6 forcefully expounds one of the central tenets of faithfulness: "Hear, O Israel: The LORD is our God, the LORD alone. You shall love the LORD your God with all your heart, and with all your soul, and with all your might. Keep these words" (Deut. 6:4–6a). The invitation to hear also provides the prelude for the Ten Commandments: "Hear, O Israel, the statutes and ordinances that I am addressing to you today; you shall learn them and observe them diligently. The LORD our God made a covenant with us at Horeb" (5:1–2).

The longing to live in the presence of this speaking God moved the Israelites to construct the tent of meeting in the wilderness as they journeyed from Egypt to Canaan. Once God had spoken to the Israelites, revealing the law, the tent was constructed. The tent was the locus of God's speaking presence. Through voice, there was a disclosure of God's purpose. It was a meeting place, not a monument to God, that could be filled with the presence of God in dialogue with humanity.[1]

As the book of Deuteronomy unfolds, it becomes clear that it is important for the people to continue to hear the voice. This constant refrain is usually translated "obey the voice." While the words *obey* and *hear* are related in several languages, to translate *shema* simply as "obey" misses the important element of relationship present between the people and God. It is more helpful to consider this phrase as an invitation to the people to stay in the presence of the God who had once spoken from atop the mountain. "Hear God's voice" is an invitation to stay close, to stay in relationship, to stay face-to-face with God.

Just as compelling are the cries from the psalmists who want God to hear their voices. "Have mercy upon me, and hear my prayer" (Ps. 4:1, KJV). "Incline thine ear unto me, and hear my speech" (17:6, KJV). "Hear, O LORD, when I cry" (27:7). "Hear, O LORD, and have mercy" (30:10, KJV). In many phrases, the psalmist repeats: "Hear my cry, my voice, my prayer, my supplications." The worshipers want God to hear their pleas and be aware of their distress. They want some assurance that God knows about their plights. In the psalms, they find the assurance through worship and ritual and oftentimes through the words of the priest who brings words of comfort and hope, words that remind them that they have not been forgotten.

God sends messengers to cry out to the people; God longs for the people to hear God's voice. And the people cry out to God longing for God to hear the words that they are speaking. We witness such a great need for relationship and understanding—from both God and people.

(Pronounce "t-loon-nohth")

Murmurings

It is not a word used many times in the Old Testament, but it delights and intrigues us. Perhaps it is because we so clearly see ourselves and our faith communities reflected in it. Although the Israelites traveling through the wilderness are separated from us by millennia, it is as if time and distance fade and we find ourselves with them standing at the door of their tents. And we murmur.

It happens so quickly. The Israelites leave the country of Egypt and experience the miraculous crossing of the Red Sea. Barely have we had time to hear Moses and then Miriam sing about the wondrous exploits of God, who has delivered them. With their songs still "hanging in the air," the people begin their murmuring.

> Then Moses ordered Israel to set out from the Red Sea, and they went into the wilderness of Shur. They went three days in the wilderness and found no water. When they came to Marah, they could not drink the water of Marah because it was bitter. That is why it was called Marah. And the people complained [murmured] against Moses, saying, "What shall we drink?" (Ex. 15:22–24)

Three days into what was to become their forty-year adventure, they murmur. The water is bitter. They ask Moses what they should drink. Yahweh shows Moses a piece of wood; Moses throws it into the water, and it becomes sweet.

At the next stop the Israelites begin murmuring once again to Moses and to Aaron. "If only we had died by the hand of [Yahweh] in the land of Egypt, when we sat by the fleshpots and ate our fill of bread; for you have brought us out into this wilderness to kill this whole assembly with hunger" (16:3). Just as Yahweh had provided the sweet water to quench the Israelites' thirst, Yahweh supplies bread for them in the morning and quail in the twilight. The storyteller wants the hearer to know that Yahweh has heard the complainings of the people and has satisfied their needs.

This is not the only story about the murmuring Israelites. There is another in the book of Numbers (the stories regarded the murmurings are found in Exodus 15, 16, 17 and Numbers 14, 16, 17). The hardships that the people are facing in the wilderness weigh heavily on them, and again they begin murmuring to Moses.

> "Would that we had died in the land of Egypt! Or that we had died in this wilderness! Why is [Yahweh] bringing us into this land to fall by the sword? Our

wives and our little ones will become booty; would it not be better for us to go back to Egypt?" So they said to one another, "Let us choose a captain, and go back to Egypt." (Num. 14:2–4)

The stories regarding the Israelites' complaints vary slightly from one another. Sometimes the people are complaining only about and to Moses, though it is made clear that ultimately this complaint is to Yahweh, who has chosen Moses to be their leader. Sometimes it is the whole traveling community, but once in Numbers it seems to be only a few or a small group of families who seem to be discontent. In some stories the murmuring is not actually about the lack of food or water that the people are experiencing. The complaints are more substantive; they involve an open rebellion to the plans and purposes of Yahweh for them. The people want to deny the calling God has given them, pack up, and return to Egypt. We can understand Yahweh's angry response to their lack of vision and trust and their tragic lack of faith.[1] What is to be learned here? Perhaps it is that Yahweh continues to lend aid to the Israelites *in spite of* their rebellion, and Israel continues to rebel *in spite of* Yahweh's aid!

(Pronounce "toh-rah")

Instruction, Teaching, Law

Psalm 119 uses the word *torah* twenty-five times, and its reading provides for us an excellent sense of the meaning, value, beauty, and significance of this word. The psalm begins with these words: "Happy are those whose way is blameless, who walk in the law of the LORD" (v. 1). The law brings satisfaction and provides direction, and it is given by Yahweh. There are many synonyms for this word *law* throughout the psalm, or at least related terms that give us a fuller sense of the kind of life and direction the psalmist treasures. Those who are happy keep decrees, seek with the heart, walk in God's ways, keep precepts and statutes, fix eyes on the commandments, praise with an upright heart, learn righteous ordinances, guard ways according to God's word, do not stray from commandments, treasure the word, do not sin, and declare ordinances. These are summarized in verses 15–16: "I will meditate on your precepts, and fix my eyes on your ways. I will delight in your statutes; I will not forget your word." It is as if the goal of the life of this one who speaks is to pray and understand the way of God in this world and to seek direction for his life. It is the psalmist's unbounded desire and longing. The psalmist wants to turn away from all that is "vanity" and not of much consequence in the world; he wants to focus on what is good and life-producing. The 176 verses of the psalm reinforce the notion that God, motivated by steadfast love, reveals to us how we should live with one another and how we should live in relation to God and the covenant we have entered. Teaching or instruction is revealed to us.

This word that means "instruction" or "law" can refer to any set of regulations. For instance, Exodus 12 contains the law in regard to observing the Passover. There are also laws for offerings, leprosy, and jealousy. The law is, in one respect, a list of ordinances, commandments, and precepts, but it is much more. In Deuteronomy, we begin to sense that the law does more than define our behavior; it is concerned with our motives, our attitudes, our hearts.

The law in Deuteronomy is more than a list of "rights and wrongs" that are handed down on tablets of stone, memorized, and hung on the classroom wall. The law has a "living quality."

In Deuteronomy, Moses' farewell address so to speak, he remembers for the people the moment when they were standing at Mount Horeb and the law was given to them. He remembers the voice of God as God spoke in the past, but he retells the story so that the hearers can realize that the covenant is of the now. Note these words and phrases being used in chapter 5: "With us," "we," "these ones," "here today," "all of us living." The text uses seven words, one used immediately after the other, to stress the contemporary claims of the law upon the lives of those listening.[1] When God is rendered as the voice that speaks, the remembering of the story in Deuteronomy is not a longing for the past; rather, the remembering is a reminder that God is capable of speaking to each and every generation—and does, in order to sustain the life of the covenant claims. Voice is an indication to the community that God is living, that God is still present with them even as they prepare for life in a new place with new challenges.[2] This understanding is conveyed here:

> The voice that goes forth from above does not reach the physical ear of man. There is no speech, there are not words; the voice is not heard. It is uttered not in sounds but in thoughts, in signs that man must learn to perceive. All the longings to return to God that come to man as well as all his inner awakenings of either joy or fear are due to that voice. Hear, O Israel. Every day a voice goes out of Mount Horeb, which the righteous men perceive. Hear, O Israel, means hear the voice that proclaims all the time, at every moment. Every day he who is worthy receives the Torah standing at Sinai, he hears the Torah from the mouth of the Lord as Israel did when they stood at Sinai. Every Israelite is able to attain this level, this level of standing at Sinai.[3]

This is an important understanding of the law, of instruction. Deuteronomy itself is cast as Moses' interpretation of the past event at Mount Horeb. Moses speaks of the importance of the historic event to the present community, a community not now standing at the foot of the mountain but now at the edge of the river. In addition, this story is told by theologians centuries later who are trying to understand the importance for their own generation. And then we read the story, and through our own hearts and minds we try to understand its importance to our own communities. The law is not static and confined; it is rich and multivalent. It calls forth a multitude of voices in different generations to embody it and give it life.

It is right, I think, to end this book with the word *torah.* Over the centuries Jewish communities have understood that interpretation of the law must be ongoing; we must try to discern the understanding of the law and interpret it in light of our own lives. So the communities have kept and gathered together the interpretations of the laws made by the teachers of their faiths, and we have included some of their thoughts and insights here. We have learned from just a few of the voices of the past. In their own words perhaps we can come to sense the richness and beauty of the Torah and the study of it. It is a gift from God.

> The world endures because of three activities: study of Torah, divine worship, and deeds of loving kindness.[4]

> Words of Torah are life to those who find them.[5]

> These are the activities whose income a man can enjoy in this world but whose principal remains undiminished for him in the world to come: honoring father and mother, deeds of loving-kindness, making peace between a man and his fellow. The study of Torah, however, equals all of these put together.[6]

> Turn to it, and turn to it again, for everything is in it. Pour over it, grow old and gray over it. Do not budge from it. You can have no better guide for living than it.[7]

> The study of Torah ranks above the building of the Temple; The study of Torah ranks above honoring father and mother; The study of Torah ranks above the saving of lives; Torah ranks above priesthood and royalty.[8]

It is my hope that we would all have this kind of love for and delight in this kind of learning. This kind of learning means wrestling with the biblical text in light of our own contexts and coming to understand all its many meanings. This kind of learning can be ultimately satisfying because we know that the "ways" of God are ultimately life-giving and abundant. The challenge is great, because the text is written in a place and time not our own. Consequently, some of its teachings must be challenged and rendered anew for our generation and those to come so that the way can be made "wide" and so that we can each find our ways to fulfillment.

For those in the Christian community the invitation will be to see how these very important words from the Old Testament are given a new context in the New. Translated from Hebrew to Greek they take on a new life; new understandings are formed and fashioned as people try to understand the ministry of Jesus in light of his and their traditions. The picture becomes more complex and intriguing.

Here we have only made a start, a beginning. But hopefully the love of learning and the love of God and the hope for a better world will keep us engaged in the challenge of simply trying to understand. A noted Jewish scholar has put it this way:

> At Sinai we received both the word and the spirit to understand the word. Some of that original understanding and response of Israel was poured into words, conveyed from mouth to mouth, entrusted in writing, but much of which words were only reflection, remained unsaid, unwritten, a tradition transmitted from soul to soul, inherited like the power to love and kept alive by constant communion with the Word, by studying it, by guarding it, by living it and by being ready to die for it. In the hands of many peoples it becomes a book, in the life of Israel it remained a voice, a Torah within the heart.[9]

Study Questions

This guide can be used by the preacher who finds one of the thirty-eight Hebrew words in the text from which she is preaching. The word might also be the starting point for a series of sermons that focuses on Hebrew words and their meanings. Such sermons could teach and inspire the community in many ways. This guide could be used by a group of clergy or laity in the church; each week the member of a study group could choose a word to explore with the others, a word that might be particularly challenging or intriguing to him.

Words are important. We explain the world and our place in it with words. Words result from our particular ways of seeing, our thoughts, and our choice of language. Words become the first utterances or sounds that the listening audience will hear. They will be used to inform, inspire, instruct, motivate, chastise, or comfort. Hence, words and their sequence help to organize the listening audience in particular ways, conveying meaning and suggesting action. They offer possibilities. They give us a common frame of reference and a way of construing the world so that we can build together. This volume has introduced us to certain words, such as light, enemy, anger, ashes, earth, and so forth. These words enable the preacher and the laity to think about the biblical text in certain ways. Thinking about these words can enhance the sermon and the task of preaching.

However this book and its study guide are used, it would be good for the reader to ask some general questions about his or her context.

Who are we as together we learn and study?

Who are we as a congregation, society, or nation, and where are we headed?

What in the world is God doing in the biblical text and in the context of our living?

123

How do we identify with each of these words? What has each meant to us in the past? now? Does this word engage us? offend us?

How might the words in this volume enable respect and care for the world?

Think about each of these words. Study them. Pray with them. See where the journey takes you.

Light

1. Where are the sources of light in your own world?
2. What does light enable you to see?
3. What is light's relationship to darkness in your life and in your relationships?
4. When has an "internal light" carried you through difficult or disturbing times?
5. When have you hidden the light? When have you been the light to others?

Enemy

1. Who is your enemy or who are the enemies in your life and in your relationships?
2. Are the enemies inside or outside you?
3. What might be the beneficial role of enemies in your life?
4. How do you recognize when you are the enemy in your relationships with self, children, other adults, or institutions?
5. What are the perceived benefits or liabilities of showing compassion to the enemy?

Anger

1. What is anger? What makes you angry?
2. How does anger motivate us to do or to be?
3. What positive functions or roles might anger play in our lives and relationships?
4. How might anger help us grow toward maturity, and how does it inhibit growth toward maturity?
5. What would a positive relationship between spirituality and anger look like?

6. How comfortable are you with the biblical texts that portray God as an angry God?
7. Are there things that happen in this world that rightfully anger God?

Ashes

1. What do ashes represent to you?
2. What symbol or metaphor is the "opposite" of ashes?
3. Why is grief important?

Earth, Land

1. What "on earth" is God doing?
2. How is the word *earth* different from the word *world* to you?
3. What is happening to our earth?
4. To whom does the earth belong, and how do we decide?
5. What does it mean to you that we come from and return to the same earth?

Fire

1. What are your earliest positive memories of fire?
2. What are your earliest negative memories of fire?
3. Think of all the various references to fire in the biblical text. What first comes to your mind?
4. How is fire used in folklore and mythology?
5. Judgment, life, and protection are some of the associations with fire in the biblical text.
   Does fire have the same associations for us today?
6. If fiery determination (compassion, caring, and judgment) are a part of the prophets' makeup, who then is taking the risk to lead us in this way today? Who are the fiery voices of our time?

To Create

1. How do you think of yourself as a cocreator with God?
2. What are the limits of your creative power?
3. How is your own power to create related to God's creativity?

4. Is God still creating in the world?
5. How is God's creativity constrained by human frailty?

Covenant

1. What does the word *covenant* mean to you?
2. What kind of covenants are you a part of today? What holds them together?
3. When are we "breaking" our covenant with God?
4. Does God ever break the covenant with us?

Blessing

1. What does it mean to be blessed? Are you?
2. Blessing is often associated with naming. Have you ever known someone who was blessed with a new name?
3. Do we need "blessing" to live healthy and productive lives?

Redeemer

1. What made the biblical use of the term *redeemer* significant?
2. Who is the "redeemer" in your family? in your church? That is, who delivers the family when it is in trouble? Who delivers the church?
3. How has God been the redeemer in your life?

Stranger

1. What does the word *stranger* mean to you? When have you been a stranger? When have there been strangers in your midst?
2. What forces turn people who were once familiar into strangers?
3. Why bother with hospitality to strangers?
4. What cultures, customs, or people do we regard as "strange"?
5. What does the stranger reveal to us about our own culture?
6. What resources do you draw from when you are the stranger?

Exile

1. What does the term *exile* mean to you?
2. What are some of the burdens of exiles?
3. Who are the exiles from the contemporary church?
4. What is our relationship to and responsibility for these exiles?
5. Are you exiled from relationships that are important to you?

Word

1. What does the phrase "word of God" mean to you?
2. What are some of the most important words in your family? in your church? in your world?
3. How do words limit us? When did you have an experience that was difficult to describe in words?
4. Where in the world do we find God's word for our lives?

Silence

1. What does silence mean to you at this time in your life?
2. How was silence used in your family?
3. What are the different kinds of silences?
4. Are you comfortable with silence?
5. Is it important for you to have silence when you worship?
6. When is it important to keep silent?
7. What is the relationship of God to silence?

To Remember

1. To remember or recall can be an exhilarating or a depressing experience. What is the importance of memory to your life? to your religious community?
2. What are your earliest memories?
3. What are your earliest memories related to church/worship?
4. What does it mean to you that God remembers?
5. What lessons of history are good for you to remember?

Sin

1. When did you first learn about the word *sin*?
2. How has this word changed, developed, or diminished in your thinking over the years?
3. How important is it that we talk in our churches about sin?
4. How is sin related or not related to illness, pathology, punishment, or misfortune?
5. What is the relationship of sin to evil and suffering?

Wisdom

1. Who were the wise persons in your family as you grew up? in your schools? in your church?
2. What are the hallmarks of a wise person?
3. What wisdom sayings or proverbs have guided your spiritual journey?
4. How might silence, remembering, sin, and wisdom be related in your religious understandings?

Steadfast Love

1. Who in your life has shown you steadfast love?
2. What images come to mind when you think of steadfast love?
3. When have you shown steadfast love?
4. What are some of the contemporary challenges to steadfast love?
5. How might steadfast love become a healing force across religious and cultural divisions?
6. What might be some of the abuses of steadfast love?

Fear

1. What are your earliest memories of fear? Who or what did you fear?
2. What can transform fear?
3. When have you overcome a fear?
4. What experiences have you had with "grace that taught my heart to fear"?
5. What people and/or social groups did you fear most as a child?
6. What does it mean to you to "fear" God?

7. When does fear immobilize you, and when does it spur you to action?

Salvation

1. What are your earliest memories of the word *salvation*?
2. How has your mind changed about salvation over the years?
3. What are some of the secular forms of salvation, and how are they offered?
4. Is there anything confusing to you about salvation?
5. From your perspective, does Christianity offer the only path to salvation?
6. How does salvation in the Bible help or hinder understandings of other, non-Christian traditions?
7. How can our understanding of salvation lead us to be respectful of other traditions?

Heart

1. What are some of the biblical understandings of "heart"?
2. What for you is the "heart" of the biblical message?
3. What does it mean to give your heart to someone?
4. What does giving your heart to God require?
5. What is the role of reason in matters of the heart?

Water

1. Water is elemental to life. It is the source of energy and rejuvenation. It takes many forms and is a metaphor for spirituality. What does it mean to you?
2. What stories do you have about your experiences with water?
3. What is the story of your baptism?

Manna

1. Have you ever experienced extreme hunger or worried about starvation?
2. What does manna or bread mean to you?
3. What are some early memories related to bread?
4. How does your thinking or activity around manna link you with those who are starving?

5. What might be a symbol for nourishment in cultures where people do not eat bread?

Justice

1. What are the biblical understandings of justice, and how do they challenge or constrain our constructions of justice today?
2. What does the phrase "justice system" mean to you?
3. How is justice talked about in your community?
4. What memories do you have of injustice?
5. How can justice avoid being oppressive or merciless?
6. What are the challenges to act with justice when we consider poorer nations and neighborhoods?

To Forgive

1. What biblical teachings about forgiveness do you find most difficult to accept?
2. Which teachings offer you the greatest hope?
3. Is it important to forgive? If yes, why? If no, why not?
4. What are your earliest memories of forgiveness?
5. What are your experiences of forgiveness with children, parents, friends, partners?
6. When do you offer or withhold forgiveness?
7. What would be an example of premature forgiveness?
8. What would be an example of mature forgiveness?
9. What are some abuses of forgiveness?

Righteousness

1. What is the righteousness that God requires of us?
2. What does it mean to be in a right relationship with God?
3. What makes living in a right relationship difficult?
4. What distinctions would you make between righteousness, self-righteousness, and righteous indignation?

To Gather

1. What are your earliest memories of family gathering places?

2. What symbols or rituals or customs are used to mark memorials?
3. What are your earliest memories of gathering for worship?
4. What do you fear most about gatherings?
5. How can gatherings be inspiring/demoralizing? What makes for the difference?
6. How does God gather us together?

Holy

1. What comes to mind when you hear this word?
2. How is the word *holy* used in the Bible?
3. How would you describe your experiences with the "Holy"?

To Wait

1. What challenges does the Bible offer to us about waiting?
2. How do you feel about waiting?
3. When is waiting a form of abuse or a waste of time?
4. When is waiting a spiritual discipline?
5. How does waiting influence your relationship to God?
6. What did family members teach you about waiting?
7. What can you learn from other non-Western cultures about waiting?
8. What healing can come from waiting?

Spirit

1. What does the word *spirit* mean to you?
2. When and how was the word introduced to you?
3. How do you interpret this word to children?
4. What is the work of the spirit in contemporary life?
5. When do you know if a spirit is evil?

To Have Compassion

1. What does the word *compassion* mean to you?
2. Would you equate the word *compassion* with love?
3. What is the opposite of compassion?
4. How is your understanding of compassion related to the understanding of "suffering with"?

To Heal

1. What does the word *healing* mean to you in today's world?
2. How is healing or wholeness possible in a fragmented and violent society such as the United States?
3. What does it mean to be "broken"?
4. How do you relate to or understand biblical stories of healing?

To Cease or Rest

1. What value was placed on "rest" in your family?
2. If you are a workaholic, how can you imagine your close relationships would change if you were not?
3. How is rest related to spirituality?
4. What is your understanding of the Sabbath?
5. Were there laws that "governed" your Sunday activities as you grew up?

To Return

1. In what ways might the word *return* be associated with spirituality or religious experience in your life?
2. To what places of spiritual significance would you return if you could?
3. How is the word *return* related to the word *repent*?
4. What stories could you share about those who turned away from God and later returned? What turned them away, and what brought them back?

Peace

1. How was peace kept in your family?
2. Who in your family were the peacemakers? the peacekeepers? the peacebreakers?
3. How is peace made or maintained?
4. Where do you turn to find or create peace in your life?
5. When is peacemaking undesirable or unwanted?
6. When is conflict or discord preferred to peacemaking?
7. How is peacemaking related to justice?

8. Is peace a realistic goal in the world?
9. In what ways is the United States a peacemaking/peacebreaking nation?

To Hear

1. What distinctions do you make between hearing and listening?
2. What sounds do you remember hearing most frequently as a child?
3. What kind of messages do you want people to hear from you?
4. What does it mean that God is a listening/speaking God?
5. How has God spoken to you in your life? Has God ever been silent? Do you imagine that God is with you in that silence?

Murmurings

1. How are murmurings dealt with in your congregation?
2. How were murmurings dealt with in your family growing up?
3. What place does murmuring have in the life of the spirit and in religious commitment?
4. What are some of the positive and negative functions of murmuring?
5. How might murmuring be related to prayer in your life or that of your congregation?
6. How might murmurings be distinguished from gossip or rumors?
7. How does murmuring lead to creative action in your setting?

Instruction, Teaching, Law

1. What instructions or teachings in the Bible are most important to you?
2. What were the most important instructions imparted to you as a child?

3. What did your mentors teach or instruct?
4. Who were the law enforcers or lawbreakers in your family?
5. How do you know when a law or teaching ceases to be compelling, relevant, or helpful?

Notes

Introduction

[1]Jewish rabbis have read and interpreted the Hebrew Bible over the centuries. Their insights have been recorded; they have enlightened and inspired many. Different bodies of material were collected over time and now are a rich resource for those who read and study the Hebrew Bible/Old Testament. The Talmud consists of two parts: The Mishnah and its commentary. The Mishnah was compiled in about 200 C.E. There are two commentaries—the Babylonian and the Palestinan. The Mishnah contains the oral law as it has been handed down from the time of the Bible. See Hershel Revel, "Talmud," in *The Universal Jewish Encyclopedia: An Authoritative and Popular Presentation of Jews and Judaism since the Earliest Times*, ed. Isaac Landman, 10 vols. (New York: Universal Jewish Encyclopedia, 1939–43), 2:160.

Midrash comes from the Hebrew word meaning "to search" or "to investigate." In midrash, the rabbis attempt a minute examination and broad interpretation of biblical texts. Sometimes the rabbis try to define more clearly the meaning of the text. Sometimes they try to expound the deeper meaning of the text in order to answer the questions and face the problems and needs of those living in later centuries. The rabbis, who accepted the Bible as a guide to life, endeavored to find expressed or implied in the text answers to life's issues and dilemmas. See Israel Bettan, "Midrash," in *Universal Jewish Encyclopedia*, 7:538.

Many of the rabbinical stories in this volume are drawn from H. N. Bialik and Y. H. Ravnitzky, *The Book of Legends* (New York: Schocken, 1992).

Light

[1]Sverre Aalen, "Light," in *Theological Dictionary of the Old Testament*, ed. G. Johannes Botterweck and Helmer Ringgren, trans. John T. Willis, 11 vols. (Grand Rapids, Mich.: Eerdmans, 1977), 1:151.

[2]Herbert Wolf, "אוֹר," in *Theological Wordbook of the Old Testament*, ed. R. Laird Harris, Gleason L. Archer, Jr., and Bruce K. Waltke, 2 vols. (Chicago: Moody Press, 1980), 1:25.

[3]"Great Is Thy Faithfulness," *Chalice Hymnal*, ed. Daniel B. Merrick and David P. Polk (St. Louis: Chalice Press, 1995), no. 86.

[4]"We Are Walking in the Light of God," *Chalice Hymnal*, no. 442.

[5]A Hasidic tale.

[6]Hasidic Judaism is a strand of Jewish thought and practice. Its essential elements concern the high importance given to mysticism. Reverence is given to the leaders of its many sects. It began in Poland in the eighteenth century; many Hasidic Jews died during the Holocaust. From "Your Guide to the Religions of the World," BBC World Service.

[7]See Louis I. Newman, ed., *The Hasidic Anthology: Tales and Teachings of the Hasidim* (Northdale, N.J.: Jason Aronson, 1987).

Enemy

[1]Helmer Ringgren, "אִיב," in *Theological Dictionary of the Old Testament*, ed. G. Johannes Botterweck and Helmer Ringgren, trans. John T. Willis, 11 vols. (Grand Rapids, Mich.: Eerdmans, 1977), 1:215.

[2]T. R. Hobbs and P. K. Jackson, "The Enemy in the Psalms," *Biblical Theology Bulletin* 21 (Spring 1991): 27.

[3]Wolfgang Roth, "Deuteronomic Rest Theology: A Redaction-Critical Study," *Biblical Research* 21 (1976): 5–14.

[4]H. N. Bialik and Y. H. Ravnitzky, *The Book of Legends* (New York: Schocken, 1992), 459.

[5]Ibid., 646.

Anger

[1]H. N. Bialik and Y. H. Ravnitzky, *The Book of Legends* (New York: Schocken, 1992), 706.

[2]Ibid., 707.

[3]Ibid.

[4]Ibid.

[5]Ibid.

[6]"The Control of Wrath," in *The Hasidic Anthology: Tales and Teachings of the Hasidim,* ed. Louis I. Newman (Northdale, N.J.: Jason Aronson, 1987), 12.

[7]Zelig Pliskin, *Consulting the Wise: Simulated Interviews with Great Torah Scholars of Previous Generations* (Brooklyn: Benei Yakov, 1991), 87.

[8]Chaim Pearl, *Theology in Rabbinic Stories* (Peabody, Mass.: Hendrickson, 1997), 108–9.

[9]William B. Silverman, *Rabbinic Stories for Christian Ministers and Teachers* (New York: Abingdon Press, 1958), 36.

Ashes

[1]William B. Silverman, *Rabbinic Stories for Christian Ministers and Teachers* (New York: Abingdon Press, 1958), 49–50.

Earth, Land

[1]Ernst Jenni and Claus Westermann, eds., *Theological Lexicon of the Old Testament,* trans. Mark E. Biddle, 3 vols. (Peabody, Mass.: Hendrickson, 1997), 1:175–77.

Fire

[1]H. N. Bialik and Y. H. Ravnitzky, *The Book of Legends* (New York: Schocken, 1992), 62.

[2]Ibid., 63.

[3]Ibid.

To Create

[1]Chaim Pearl, *Theology in Rabbinic Stories* (Peabody, Mass.: Hendrickson, 1997), 7.

[2]Ernst Jenni and Claus Westermann, eds., *Theological Lexicon of the Old Testament,* trans. Mark E. Biddle, 3 vols. (Peabody, Mass.: Hendrickson, 1997), 1:255.

Covenant

[1]Chaim Pearl, *Theology in Rabbinic Stories* (Peabody, Mass.: Hendrickson, 1997), 13.

Blessing

[1]The interpretive question regarding Jacob is drawn from Athanasios Hatzopoulos, "The Struggle for a Blessing: Reflections on Genesis 32:24–31," *The Ecumenical Review* (Oct. 1996): 507–12.

Redeemer

[1]H. N. Bialik and Y. H. Ravnitzky, *The Book of Legends* (New York: Schocken, 1992), 390.

Stranger

[1]H. N. Bialik and Y. H. Ravnitzky, *The Book of Legends* (New York: Schocken, 1992), 679.
[2]Ibid., 34.

Exile

[1]Ada Maria Isasi-Diaz, "'By the Rivers of Babylon: Exile As a Way of Life," in *Reading from This Place: Social Location and Biblical Interpretation in the United States*, ed. Fernando F. Segovia and Mary Ann Tolbert (Minneapolis: Fortress Press, 1995), 149–64.
[2]H. N. Bialik and Y. H. Ravnitzky, *The Book of Legends* (New York: Schocken, 1992), 377.
[3]Ibid.

Silence

[1]William B. Silverman, *Rabbinic Stories for Christian Ministers and Teachers* (New York: Abingdon Press, 1958), 71.
[2]Barbara Brown Taylor, *When God Is Silent* (Cambridge, Mass: Cowley, 1998), 80.
[3]H. N. Bialik and Y. H. Ravnitzky, *The Book of Legends* (New York: Schocken, 1992), 704.

Sin

[1]H. N. Bialik and Y. H. Ravnitzky, *The Book of Legends* (New York: Schocken, 1992), 545.
[2]Ibid., 538.
[3]Ibid.
[4]Ibid.
[5]Ibid., 583.

Wisdom

[1]H. N. Bialik and Y. H. Ravnitzky, *The Book of Legends* (New York: Schocken, 1992), 469.
[2]Ibid., 470.
[3]Gerhard von Rad, *Wisdom in Israel* (Valley Forge, Pa.: Trinity Press International, 1972), 62.

Steadfast Love

[1]William B. Silverman, *Rabbinic Stories for Christian Ministers and Teachers* (New York: Abingdon Press, 1958), 33.
[2]Dr. Martin Luther King, Jr., *Where Do We Go From Here: Chaos or Community?* (Boston: Beacon Press, 1989), 89–90.
[3]"O Love, That Wilt Not Let Me Go," *Chalice Hymnal*, ed. Daniel B. Merrick and David P. Polk (St. Louis: Chalice Press, 1995), no. 540.

Fear

[1]"Amazing Grace!" *Chalice Hymnal*, ed. Daniel B. Merrick and David P. Polk (St. Louis: Chalice Press, 1995), no. 546.

Salvation

[1]John F. A. Sawyer, "יֵשַׁע," in *Theological Dictionary of the Old Testament*, ed. G. Johannes Botterweck and Helmer Ringgren, trans. John T. Willis, 11 vols. (Grand Rapids, Mich.: Eerdmans, 1977), 6:445.

[2]Ibid., 450.

[3]H. N. Bialik and Y. H. Ravnitzky, *The Book of Legends* (New York: Schocken, 1992), 72.

[4]Sawyer, 6:459.

[5]John E. Hartley, "יֵשַׁע," in *Theological Wordbook of the Old Testament*, ed. R. Laird Harris, Gleason L. Archer, Jr., and Bruce K. Waltke, 2 vols. (Chicago: Moody Press, 1980), 1:414.

Heart

[1]Heinz-Josef Fabry, "לֵב," in *Theological Dictionary of the Old Testament*, ed. G. Johannes Botterweck and Helmer Ringgren, trans. John T. Willis, 11 vols. (Grand Rapids, Mich.: Eerdmans, 1977), 7:411-22.

[2]Ibid., 411.

[3]Ibid., 414.

[4]Ibid., 422.

[5]H. N. Bialik and Y. H. Ravnitzky, *The Book of Legends* (New York: Schocken, 1992), 509.

[6]Howard Thurman, *The Centering Moment* (Richmond, Ind.: Friends United Press, 1976), 35.

Water

[1]H. N. Bialik and Y. H. Ravnitzky, *The Book of Legends* (New York: Schocken, 1992), 588.

[2]R. E. Clements, "מַיִם,"in *Theological Dictionary of the Old Testament*, ed. G. Johannes Botterweck and Helmer Ringgren, trans. John T. Willis, 11 vols. (Grand Rapids, Mich.: Eerdmans, 1977), 8:278–80.

[3]Bialik and Ravnitzky, *Book of Legends*, 261.

[4]Walter C. Kaiser, "מַיִם," in *Theological Wordbook of the Old Testament*, ed. R. Laird Harris, Gleason L. Archer, Jr., and Bruce K. Waltke, 2 vols. (Chicago: Moody Press, 1980), 1:1188.

Manna

[1]"Guide Me, O Thou Great Jehovah," *Chalice Hymnal*, ed. Daniel B. Merrick and David P. Polk (St. Louis: Chalice Press, 1995), no. 622.

Justice

[1]William B. Silverman, *Rabbinic Stories for Christian Ministers and Teachers* (New York: Abingdon Press, 1958), 35.

To Forgive

[1]J. J. Stamm, "סלח," in *Theological Lexicon of the Old Testament*, ed. Ernst Jenni and Claus Westermann, trans. Mark Biddle (Peabody, Mass.: Hendrickson, 1997), 1:797–99.

Righteousness

[1]J. Patton, "Righteousness," in *Dictionary of Pastoral Care and Counseling*, ed. Rodney J. Hunter (Nashville: Abingdon Press, 1990), 1087.

[2]H. N. Bialik and Y. H. Ravnitzky, *The Book of Legends* (New York: Schocken, 1992), 548.

[3]Ibid., 548.

[4]Ibid., 549.

Holy

[1]"Holy, Holy, Holy! Lord God Almighty!" *Chalice Hymnal*, ed. Daniel B. Merrick and David P. Polk (St. Louis: Chalice Press, 1995), no. 4.

[2]"Take Time to Be Holy," *Chalice Hymnal*, no. 572.

To Wait

[1]Alex Ayres, ed. *The Wisdom of Martin Luther King, Jr.: An A to Z Guide to the Ideas and Ideals of the Great Civil Rights Leader* (New York: Meridian Books, 1993), 231.

Spirit

[1]J. W. Jennings, "Holy Spirit, Doctrine of, and Pastoral Care" in *Dictionary of Pastoral Care and Counseling*, ed. Rodney J. Hunter (Nashville: Abingdon Press, 1990), 525–26.

[2]J. Barton Payne, "רוח," *Theological Wordbook of the Old Testament*, ed. R. Laird Harris, Gleason L. Archer, Jr., and Bruce K. Waltke, 2 vols. (Chicago: Moody Press, 1980), 2:836–37.

[3]Howard Thurman, *The Centering Moment* (Richmond, Ind.: Friends United Press, 1976), 110.

To Have Compassion

[1]William B. Silverman, *Rabbinic Stories for Christian Ministers and Teachers* (New York: Abingdon Press, 1958), 37.

[2]Ibid.

To Heal

[1]D. Guernsey, "Healing," in *Dictionary of Pastoral Care and Counseling*, ed. Rodney J. Hunter (Nashville: Abingdon Press, 1990), 497.

To Cease or Rest

[1]Paul Achtemeier, *Harper's Bible Dictionary* (San Francisco: Harper and Row, 1985), 888–89.

[2]Victor P. Hamilton, "שבת," in *Theological Wordbook of the Old Testament*, ed. R. Laird Harris, Gleason L. Archer, Jr., and Bruce K. Waltke, 2 vols. (Chicago: Moody Press, 1980), 2:903.

[3]H. N. Bialik and Y. H. Ravnitzky, *The Book of Legends* (New York: Schocken, 1992), 492.

[4]Ibid., 492–93.

[5]Ibid., 465.

Peace

[1]Dennis J. McCarthy, "Psalm 85 and the Meaning of Peace," *Way* 22 (1982): 3–9.

[2]Martin Luther King, Jr., "True Peace," speech delivered July 5, 1962, in Atlanta.

To Hear

[1]Although the relationship between the tent and the tabernacle is uncertain, the tent of meeting was the location of revelation as people traveled through the wilderness. See Richard Elliott Friedman, "Tabernacle," in *Anchor Bible Dictionary*, ed. David Noel Freedman, 6 vols. (New York: Doubleday, 1992), 6:292–300.

Murmurings

[1]George W. Coats, *Rebellion in the Wilderness: The Murmuring Motif in the Wilderness Traditions of the Old Testament* (Nashville: Abingdon Press, 1968).

Instruction, Teaching, Law

[1]Patrick Miller, *Deuteronomy*, Interpretation (Louisville: John Knox Press, 1990), 67.

[2]Mary Donovan Turner and Mary Lin Hudson, *Saved from Silence: Finding Women's Voice in Preaching* (St. Louis: Chalice Press, 1999), 27.

[3]Abraham Heschel, *God in Search of Man* (New York: Farrar, Strauss, and Cudally, 1955), 146.

[4]H. N. Bialik and Y. H. Ravnitzky, *The Book of Legends* (New York: Schocken, 1992), 403.

[5]Ibid.

[6]Ibid.

[7]Ibid.

[8]Ibid.

[9]Heschel, *God in Search of Man,* 275.

Index of Biblical Citations

For Further Information

Several Hebrew reference tools use numbers from any of the editions of *Strong's Exhaustive Concordance*. Using these numbers, a reader can find all the occurrences of a Hebrew word in the Hebrew Bible. Listed below are the Strong's numbers for each of this book's thirty-eight Hebrew words.

Anger	639	Light	215, 216
Ashes	665	Manna	4478
Blessing	1293, 1294	Murmurings	8519
Cease, Rest	7673, 7676	Peace	7965
Covenant	1285	Redeemer	1350
Create	1254	Remember	2142
Earth, Land	776	Return	7725
Enemy	340, 341	Righteousness	6663, 6666
Exile	1540	Salvation	3444, 3467
Fear	3372, 3373	Silence	1826, 1827
Fire	784	Sin	2398, 2399
Forgive	5545	Spirit	7307
Gather	6908	Steadfast Love	2617
Have Compassion		Stranger	1481
	7355, 7356,	Wait	6960
	7358	Water	4325
Heal	7495	Wisdom	2449, 2450,
Hear	8085		2451
Heart	3820, 3824	Word	1697
Holy	6942, 6944		
Instruction, Teaching, Law			
	8451, 8452		
Justice	4941